THE FEDERAL BUDGET PROCESS: A GLOSSARY OF TERMS

THE FEDERAL BUDGET PROCESS: A GLOSSARY OF TERMS

JESSE L. GIBBLER
EDITOR

Novinka Books
An imprint of Nova Science Publishers, Inc.
New York

NOTICE TO THE READER

Library of Congress Cataloging-in-Publication Data:
The federal budget process : a glossary of terms / Jesse L. Gibbler (editor).
    p. cm.
Originally published: A glossary of terms used in the federal budget process. Rev. [1993]
Includes index.
ISBN 1-60021-148-8
1. Budget--United States--Dictionaries. 2. Budget process--United States--Dictionaries. 3. Finance, Public--United States--Dictionaries. I. Gibbler, Jesse L. II. Glossary of terms used in the federal budget process.
HJ2051.G564   2006
352.4'8097303--dc22   2006009916

Published by Nova Science Publishers, Inc. ✤ New York

CONTENTS

PREFACE

The federal budget process is the primary means by which the President and Congress select among competing demands for federal funds. The President's budget is the Administration's proposed plan for managing funds, setting levels of spending, and financing the spending of the federal government. It is not only the President's principal policy statement but is also the starting point for congressional budgetary actions. The budget's importance makes it essential that it be comprehensive and clear.

This glossary provides standard terms, definitions, and classifications for the government's fiscal, budget, and program information. It was developed in cooperation with the Secretary of the Treasury and the Directors of the Office of Management and Budget (OMB) and the Congressional Budget Office (CBO). This glossary is a basic reference document for the Congress, federal agencies, and others interested in the federal budget-making process. Like previous editions, this revision emphasizes budget terms, but relevant economic and accounting terms are also defined to help the user appreciate the dynamics of the budget process and its relationship to other key activities (e.g., financial reporting). It also distinguishes between any differences in budgetary and nonbudgetary meanings of terms.

All terms in the 1993 Exposure Draft were reviewed and additions, revisions, or deletions made. We added a number of performance budgeting-related terms and deleted Budget Enforcement Act terms that are no longer relevant.

The *Glossary* is by no means an exhaustive list of terms related to the budget. We decided to include only those commonly used terms that are most significant in the congressional and executive budget processes. Executive, legislative, and other budget experts participated in the selections and definitions of the *Glossary* terms. While every effort was made to resolve differences, the final selections and definitions were made by GAO. The *Glossary* can be accessed online at www.gao.gov.

David M. Walker
Comptroller General of the United States

Chapter 1

GLOSSARY OF TERMS

United States Government Accountability Office

A

ACCOUNT

A separate financial reporting unit for budget, management, and/or accounting purposes. All budgetary transactions are recorded in accounts, but not all accounts are budgetary in nature. Some accounts do not directly affect the budget but are used purely for accounting purposes. Budget accounts are used to record all transfers within the budget, whereas other accounts (such as deposit fund, credit financing, and foreign currency accounts) are used for accounting purposes connected with funds that are nonbudgetary in nature. The Office of Management and Budget (OMB), in consultation with the Department of the Treasury (Treasury), assigns account identification codes reflecting appropriations as enacted in appropriations laws. Treasury establishes and maintains a system of accounts that provides the basic structure for the *U.S. Standard General Ledger* Chart of Accounts. (*See also* Accounts in the President's Budget; Accounts for Purposes Other Than Budget Presentation; Credit Reform Act Accounts *under* Federal Credit; *Standard General Ledger* Chart of Accounts.)

Appropriation Account

The basic unit of an appropriation generally reflecting each unnumbered paragraph in an appropriation act. An appropriation account typically encompasses a number of activities or projects and may be subject to restrictions or conditions applicable to only the account, the appropriation act, titles within an appropriation act, other appropriation acts, or the government as a whole. (*See also* Appropriation Rider; Continuing Appropriation/Continuing Resolution; Line Item; Supplemental Appropriation.)

ACCOUNT IN THE PRESIDENT'S BUDGET: EXPENDITURE/APPROPRIATION AND RECEIPT ACCOUNTS CLASSIFIED BY FUND TYPES

Accounts used by the federal government to record outlays (expenditure accounts) and income (receipt accounts) primarily for budgeting or management information purposes but also for accounting purposes. All budget (and off-budget) accounts are classified as being either expenditure or receipt (including offsetting receipt) accounts and by fund group. Budget (and off-budget) transactions fall within either of two fund groups: (1) federal funds and (2) trust funds.

All federal fund and trust fund accounts are included within the budget (that is, they are on-budget) unless they are excluded from the budget by law. Federal and trust funds excluded from the budget by law are classified as being off-budget. The term off-budget differs from the term nonbudgetary. Nonbudgetary refers to activities (such as the credit financing accounts) that do not belong in the budget under existing concepts, while off-budget refers to accounts that belong on-budget under budget concepts but that are excluded from the budget under terms of law.

Federal Fund AccountsBudgetary accounts composed of moneys collected and spent by the federal government other than those designated as trust funds. Federal fund accounts include general, special, public enterprise, and intragovernmental fund accounts. (*See also Standard General Ledger Chart of Accounts.*)

General Fund Accounts

Accounts in the U.S. Treasury holding all federal money not allocated by law to any other fund account.

General Fund Receipt Account

A receipt account credited with all collections that are not earmarked by law for another account for a specific purpose. These collections are presented in the President's budget as either governmental (budget) receipts or offsetting receipts. These include taxes, customs duties, and miscellaneous receipts.

General Fund Expenditure Account

An appropriation account established to record amounts appropriated by law for the general support of federal government activities and the subsequent expenditure of these funds. It includes spending from both annual and permanent appropriations.

Intragovernmental Fund Accounts

Expenditure accounts authorized by law to facilitate financing transactions primarily within and between federal agencies.

Intragovernmental Revolving Fund Account

An appropriation account authorized to be credited with collections from other federal agencies' accounts that are earmarked to finance a continuing cycle of business-type operations, including working capital funds, industrial funds, stock funds, and supply funds. According to the Office of Management and Budget (OMB), collections of intragovernmental revolving fund accounts are derived primarily from within the government. For example, the franchise fund operations within several agencies provide common administrative services to federal agencies on a fee-for-service basis. (*See also* Working Capital Fund.)

Management Fund Account

An account established by the Department of the Treasury (Treasury) that is authorized by law to credit collections from two or more appropriations to finance activity not involving a continuing cycle of business-type operations. Such accounts do not generally own a significant amount of assets, such as supplies, equipment, or loans, nor do they have a specified amount of capital provided—a corpus. The Navy Management Fund is an example of such an account.

Consolidated Working Fund Accounts are a subset of management funds. These are special working funds established under the authority of Section 601 of the Economy Act (31 U.S.C. §§ 1535, 1536) to receive advance payments from other agencies or accounts. Consolidated working fund accounts are not used to finance the work directly but only to reimburse the appropriation or fund account that will finance the work to be performed. Amounts in consolidated working fund accounts are available for the same periods as those of the accounts advancing the funds. Consolidated working fund accounts are shown as separate accounts on the books of Treasury but are not separately identified in the President's budget. Transactions of these accounts are included in the presentation of the appropriation or fund account actually performing the service or providing the materials.

Public Enterprise Revolving Fund Account

A type of revolving fund that conducts cycles of businesslike operations, mainly with the public, in which it charges for the sale of products or services and uses the proceeds to finance its spending, usually without requirement for annual appropriations. Most government corporations are financed by public enterprise funds. (*See* Revolving Fund.)

Special Fund Accounts

Federal fund accounts earmarked by law for a specific purpose.

Special Fund Receipt Account.

A receipt account credited with collections that are earmarked by law but included in the federal funds group rather than classified as trust fund collections. These collections are presented in the President's budget as either governmental (budget) receipts or offsetting receipts. (*See also* Earmarking.)

Special Fund Expenditure Account

An appropriation account established to record appropriations, obligations, and outlays financed by the proceeds of special fund receipts. (*See also* Earmarking.)

Trust Fund Accounts

Accounts designated as "trust funds" by law, regardless of any other meaning of the term "trust fund." A trust fund account is usually either a receipt, an expenditure, or a revolving fund account. Except in rare circumstances (for example, Indian Trust Funds), a trust fund account imposes no fiduciary responsibility on the federal government. For a fuller discussion of trust funds, see *Federal Trust and Other Earmarked Funds: Answers to Frequently Asked Questions* (GAO-01-199SP). (*See also* Earmarking.)

Trust Fund Expenditure Account

An appropriation account established to record appropriated amounts of trust fund receipts used to finance specific purposes or programs under a trust agreement or statute.

Trust Fund Receipt Account

A receipt account credited with collections classified as trust fund collections. These collections are recorded as either governmental receipts or offsetting receipts.

Trust Revolving Fund Account

A trust fund expenditure account that is an appropriation account authorized to be credited with collections and used, without further appropriation action, to carry out a cycle of business-type operations in accordance with statute.

ACCOUNTS FOR PURPOSES OTHER THAN BUDGET PRESENTATION

Clearing Accounts

Accounts that temporarily hold general, special, or trust fund federal government collections or disbursements pending clearance to the applicable receipt or expenditure accounts.

Deposit Fund Accounts

Nonbudgetary accounts established to account for collections that are either (1) held temporarily and later refunded or paid upon administrative or legal determination as to the proper disposition thereof or (2) held by the government, which acts as banker or agent for others, and paid out at the direction of the depositor. Examples include savings accounts for military personnel, state and local income taxes withheld from federal employees' salaries, and payroll deductions for the purchase of savings bonds by civilian employees of the government. Deposit fund balances are accounted for as liabilities of the federal government. These accounts are not included in the budget totals because the amounts are not owned by the government.

Therefore, the budget records transactions between deposit funds and budgetary accounts as transactions with the public. Deposit fund balances may be held in the form of either invested or uninvested balances. However, since the cash in the accounts is used by the Department of the Treasury to satisfy immediate cash requirements of the government, to the extent that they are not invested in federal debt, changes in uninvested deposit fund balances are shown as a means of financing the deficit in the budget.

Foreign Currency Fund Accounts

Accounts established in the Department of the Treasury for foreign currency that is acquired without payment of U.S. dollars. Examples of such accounts are those set up through the Agricultural Trade Development and Assistance Act (7 U.S.C. §§ 1691–1736g).

Suspense Accounts

Combined receipt and expenditure accounts established to temporarily hold funds that are later refunded or paid into another government fund when an administrative or final determination as to the proper disposition is made.

Transfer Appropriation (Allocation) Accounts

Accounts established to receive and disburse allocations. Such allocations and transfers are not adjustments to budget authority or balances of budget authority. Rather, the transactions and any adjustments therein are treated as nonexpenditure transfers at the time the allocations are made. The accounts carry symbols that identify the original appropriation from which moneys have been advanced. Transfer appropriation accounts are symbolized by adding the receiving agency's department prefix to the original appropriation or fund account symbol. In some cases, a bureau suffix is added to show that the transfer is being made to a particular bureau within the receiving department. For budget purposes, transactions in the transfer accounts are reported with the transactions in the parent accounts. For further information, see the *Treasury Financial Manual*. (*See also* Allocation; Nonexpenditure Transfer *under* Transfer.)

ACCOUNTS LISTED IN THE STANDARD GENERAL LEDGER

See under Standard General Ledger (SGL) Chart of Accounts.

ACCOUNTS PAYABLE

Amounts owed by a federal agency for goods and services received from, progress in contract performance made by, and rents due to other entities. This is a proprietary (or financial) accounting term. For balance sheet reporting purposes, according to OMB Circular No. A-11 "accounts payable" consists of the amount owed by the reporting entity for goods and services received from other entities, progress in contract performance made by other entities, and rents due to other entities. (*See also* Accounts Receivable; Proprietary Accounting; app. III.)

ACCOUNTS RECEIVABLE

Amounts due from others for goods furnished and services rendered. Such amounts include reimbursements earned and refunds receivable. This is a proprietary (or financial) accounting and not a budget term. Accounts receivable do not constitute budget authority against which an agency may incur an obligation. For federal proprietary accounting, accounts receivable are assets that arise from specifically identifiable, legally enforceable claims to cash or other assets through an entity's established assessment processes or when goods or services are provided. (*See also* Accounts Payable; Proprietary Accounting; app. III.)

ACCRUAL ACCOUNTING

A system of accounting in which revenues are recorded when earned and expenses are recorded when goods are received or services are performed, even though the actual receipt of revenues and payment for goods or services may occur, in whole or in part, at a different time. (*See also* Cash Accounting; app. III.)

ADMINISTRATIVE DIVISION OR SUBDIVISION OF FUNDS

Any apportionment or other distribution of an appropriation or fund made pursuant to the Antideficiency Act (31 U.S.C. §§ 1511–1519). The appropriation may be divided or subdivided administratively within the limits of the apportionment (31 U.S.C. § 1513(d)). The expenditure or obligation of the divided or subdivided appropriation or fund may not exceed the apportionment (31 U.S.C. § 1517(a)). (*See also* Antideficiency Act; Antideficiency Act Violation; Apportionment; Limitation.)

ADVANCE APPROPRIATION

Budget authority provided in an appropriation act that becomes available 1 or more fiscal years after the fiscal year for which the appropriation act was enacted. For example, a fiscal year 2005 appropriation act could provide that the budget authority for a specified activity would not become available until October 1, 2005 (the start of fiscal year 2006), or later. The amount is not included in the budget totals of the year for which the appropriation act is enacted but rather in those for the fiscal year in which the amount will become available for obligation. In the example above, the budget authority would be recorded in fiscal year 2006. (For a distinction, *see* Advance Funding; Forward Funding; Multiple-Year Authority *under* Duration *under* Budget Authority.)

ADVANCE FUNDING

Budget authority provided in an appropriation act to obligate and disburse (outlay) in the current fiscal year funds from a succeeding year's appropriation. Advance funding is a means to avoid making supplemental requests late in the fiscal year for certain entitlement programs in cases where the appropriations for the current year prove to be insufficient. When such budget authority is used (i.e., funds obligated), the budget records an increase in the budget authority for the fiscal year in which it is used and a reduction in the budget authority for the following fiscal year. (For a distinction, *see* Advance Appropriation; Multiple-Year Authority *under* Duration *under* Budget Authority; Forward Funding.)

ADVANCE PAYMENT

An amount paid prior to the later receipt of goods, services, or other assets. Advances are ordinarily made only to payees to whom an agency has an obligation, and they do not exceed the amount of the obligation.

AGENCY

No one definition of this term has general, governmentwide applicability. "Agency" and related terms, like "executive agency" or "federal agency," are defined in different ways in different laws and regulations. For example, the provisions of the Budget and Accounting Act of 1921 relating to the preparation of the President's budget specifically define "agency" to include the District of Columbia government but exclude the legislative branch or the Supreme Court (31 U.S.C. § 1101).

AGENCY MISSION

Term used in section 1105(a)(22) of title 31 of the *United States Code*, which outlines content requirements for the President's budget submission to Congress. Section 1105 requires that the President's budget contain a statement of agency budget authority in terms of agency missions, but this section offers no definition. The term is generally accepted to refer to the purpose of the programs of the agency and its component organizations. In the Office of Management and Budget's (OMB) budget functional classification system, agency missions are distinguished from national needs. National needs are generally described as major functions, while agency missions are generally described in the context of subfunctions. (*See also* Functional Classification.)

ALLOCATION

For the purposes of budgeting, an allocation means a delegation, authorized in law, by one agency of its authority to obligate budget authority and outlay funds to another agency. (The appropriation or fund from which the allocation is made is generally referred to as the parent appropriation or fund.) An allocation is made when one or more agencies share the administration of a program for which appropriations are made to only one of the agencies or to the President. When an allocation occurs, the Department of the Treasury establishes a subsidiary account called a "transfer appropriation account," and the agency receiving the allocation may obligate up to the amount included in the account. The budget does not show the transfer appropriation account separately. Transactions involving allocation accounts appear in the Object Classification Schedule, with the corresponding Program and Financing Schedule, in the President's budget. For an illustration of the treatment of Object Classification—With Allocation Accounts, see OMB Circular No. A-11. (*See also* Object Classification; Transfer; Transfer Appropriation (Allocation) Accounts *under* Account for Purposes Other Than Budget Presentation.)

For purposes of section 302(a) of the Congressional Budget and Impoundment Control Act of 1974 (2 U.S.C. § 633(a)), an allocation is the distribution of spending authority and outlays to relevant committees based on the levels contained in a concurrent resolution on the budget. (*See also* Committee Allocation.)

For purposes of section 302(b) of the Congressional Budget and Impoundment Control Act of 1974 (2 U.S.C. § 633(b)), an allocation is the distribution of spending authority and outlays to relevant subcommittees based on the levels contained in the concurrent resolution on the budget. (*See also* Subcommittee Allocation.)

For funds control purposes, an allocation is a further subdivision of an apportionment.

ALLOTMENT

An authorization by either the agency head or another authorized employee to his/her subordinates to incur obligations within a specified amount. Each agency makes allotments pursuant to specific procedures it establishes within the general apportionment requirements stated in OMB Circular No. A-11. The amount allotted by an agency cannot exceed the amount apportioned by the Office of Management and Budget (OMB). An allotment is part of an agency system of administrative control of funds whose purpose is to keep obligations and expenditures from exceeding apportionments and allotments. (*See also* Administrative Division or Subdivision of Funds; Apportionment; Reapportionment.)

ALLOWANCE

An amount included in the President's budget request or included in a projection in a congressional resolution on the budget to cover possible additional proposals, such as contingencies for programs whose expenditures are controllable only by statutory change and other requirements. As used by Congress in the concurrent resolutions on the budget, an allowance represents a special functional classification designed to include an amount to cover possible requirements. An allowance remains undistributed until the contingency on which it is based occurs; then it is distributed to the appropriate functional classification. For agency budgetary accounting and fund control purposes, an allowance is a subdivision of an allotment. For treatment of undistributed allowances, see function 920 in the table "Outlays by Function and Subfunction" in the *Historical Tables* of the President's budget. (For more details on the government accounting definition, *see Standard General Ledger* Chart of Accounts.) For federal proprietary accounting, an allowance also represents the estimated uncollectible amount of accounts receivable.

ANTIDEFICIENCY ACT

Federal law that

- prohibits the making of expenditures or the incurring of obligations in advance of an appropriation;
- prohibits the incurring of obligations or the making of expenditures in excess of amounts available in appropriation or fund accounts unless specifically authorized by law (31 U.S.C. § 1341(a));
- prohibits the acceptance of voluntary or personal services unless authorized by law (31 U.S.C. § 1342);
- requires the Office of Management and Budget (OMB), via delegation from the President, to apportion appropriated funds and other budgetary resources for all executive branch agencies (31 U.S.C. § 1512);
- requires a system of administrative controls within each agency (*see* 31 U.S.C. § 1514 for the administrative divisions established);
- prohibits incurring any obligation or making any expenditure in excess of an apportionment or reapportionment or in excess of other

subdivisions established pursuant to sections 1513 and 1514 of title 31 of the *United States Code* (31 U.S.C. § 1517); and

- specifies penalties for deficiencies (*see* Antideficiency Act Violation).

The act permits agencies to reserve funds (that is, withhold them from obligation) under certain circumstances. (*See also* Administrative Division or Subdivision of Funds; Antideficiency Act Violation; Apportionment; Budgetary Reserves; Deferral of Budget Authority; Deficiency Apportionment; Deficiency Appropriation; Expenditure; Fund Accounting; Congressional Budget and Impoundment Control Act of 1994; Outlay.)

ANTIDEFICIENCY ACT VIOLATION

Occurs when one or more of the following happens:

- overobligation or overexpenditure of an appropriation or fund account (31 U.S.C. § 1341(a));
- entering into a contract or making an obligation in advance of an appropriation, unless specifically authorized by law (31 U.S.C. § 1341(a));
- acceptance of voluntary service, unless authorized by law (31 U.S.C. § 1342); or
- overobligation or overexpenditure of (1) an apportionment or reapportionment or (2) amounts permitted by the administrative control of funds regulations (31 U.S.C. § 1517(a)).

Once it has been determined that there has been a violation of the Antideficiency Act, the agency head must report all relevant facts and a statement of actions taken to the President and Congress and submit a copy of the report to the Comptroller General. Penalties for Antideficiency Act violations include administrative discipline, such as suspension from duty without pay or removal from office. In addition, an officer or employee convicted of willfully and knowingly violating the law shall be fined not more than $5,000, imprisoned for not more than 2 years, or both (31 U.S.C. §§ 1349, 1350, 1518, and 1519). (*See also* Administrative Division or Subdivision of Funds; Antideficiency Act; Expenditure.)

APPORTIONMENT

The action by which the Office of Management and Budget (OMB) distributes amounts available for obligation, including budgetary reserves established pursuant to law, in an appropriation or fund account. An apportionment divides amounts available for obligation by specific time periods (usually quarters), activities, projects, objects, or a combination thereof. The amounts so apportioned limit the amount of obligations that may be incurred. An apportionment may be further subdivided by an agency into allotments, suballotments, and allocations. In apportioning any account, some funds may be reserved to provide for contingencies or to effect savings made possible pursuant to the Antideficiency Act. Funds apportioned to establish a reserve must be proposed for deferral or rescission pursuant to the Impoundment Control Act of 1974 (2 U.S.C. §§ 681–688).

The apportionment process is intended to (1) prevent the obligation of amounts available within an appropriation or fund account in a manner that would require deficiency or supplemental appropriations and (2) achieve the most effective and economical use of amounts made available for obligation. (*See also* Administrative Division or Subdivision of Funds; Allotment; Antideficiency Act; Appropriated Entitlement; Budgetary Reserves; Deferral of Budget Authority; Deficiency Apportionment; Deficiency Appropriation; Limitation; Reapportionment; Rescission; Supplemental Appropriation.)

APPROPRIATED ENTITLEMENT

An entitlement whose source of funding is in an annual appropriation act. However, because the entitlement is created by operation of law, if Congress does not appropriate the money necessary to fund the payments, eligible recipients may have legal recourse. Veterans' compensation and Medicaid are examples of such appropriated entitlements. (*See also* Entitlement Authority.)

APPROPRIATION ACT

A statute, under the jurisdiction of the House and Senate Committees on Appropriations, that generally provides legal authority for federal agencies to incur obligations and to make payments out of the Treasury for specified purposes. An appropriation act fulfills the requirement of Article I, Section 9, of the U.S. Constitution, which provides that "no money shall be drawn from the Treasury, but in Consequence of Appropriations made by Law." Under the rules of both houses, an appropriation act should follow enactment of authorizing legislation. (*See also* Appropriations *under* Forms of Budget Authority *under* Budget Authority; Authorizing Legislation; Limitation.)

Major types of appropriation acts are regular, supplemental, deficiency, and continuing. Regular appropriation acts are all appropriation acts that are not supplemental, deficiency, or continuing. Currently, regular annual appropriation acts that provide funding for the continued operation of federal departments, agencies, and various government activities are considered by Congress annually. From time to time, supplemental appropriation acts are also enacted. When action on regular appropriation bills is not completed before the beginning of the fiscal year, a continuing resolution (often referred to simply as "CR") may be enacted in a bill or joint resolution to provide funding for the affected agencies for the full year, up to a specified date, or until their regular appropriations are enacted. A deficiency appropriation act provides budget authority to cover obligations incurred in excess of available budget authority. (*See also* Continuing Appropriation/Continuing Resolution; Supplemental Appropriation; Deficiency Appropriation.)

APPROPRIATION RIDER

Sometimes used to refer to (1) a provision that is not directly related to the appropriation to which it is attached or (2) a limitation or requirement in an appropriation act. (*See also* Limitation.)

ASSET

Tangible or intangible items owned by the federal government, which would have probable economic benefits that can be obtained or controlled by a federal government entity. (*See also* Liability.)

ASSET SALE

The sale of a physical or financial asset owned in whole or in part by the federal government to the public. Asset sales are typically large-dollar transactions ($50 million or more) for which advance notification must be provided to the Department of the Treasury. Revenue from the sale of assets is accounted for in the budget as offsetting receipts or collections.

In general, asset sales increase current cash payments received by the government at the expense of a stream of future income that the government would otherwise receive. (*See also* Direct Loan *under* Federal Credit.)

APPROPRIATIONS

See under Forms of Budget Authority *under* Budget Authority.

AUTHORIZING COMMITTEE

A standing committee of the House or Senate with legislative jurisdiction over the establishment, continuation, and operations of federal programs or agencies. The jurisdiction of such committees extends, in addition to program legislation, to authorization of appropriations legislation. (Normally, authorization of appropriations legislation is a prerequisite for making appropriations for the given programs or agencies.) An authorizing committee also has jurisdiction in those instances where backdoor authority is provided in the substantive legislation. For further discussion, see the current rules of the House of Representatives and the Senate. (*See also* Authorizing Legislation; Backdoor Authority/Backdoor Spending; Oversight Committee; Spending Committee.)

AUTHORIZING LEGISLATION

Substantive legislation, proposed by a committee of jurisdiction other than the House or Senate Appropriations Committees, that establishes and continues the operation of a federal program or agency either indefinitely or for a specific period or that sanctions a particular type of obligation or expenditure within a program. This term is used in two different ways: (1) to describe legislation enacting new program authority, that is, authorizing the program, and (2) to describe legislation authorizing an appropriation.

Authorization of appropriations legislation authorizes the enactment of appropriations of specific amounts for specific programs and activities to be provided in an appropriation act. An authorization of appropriations is, under congressional rules, a prerequisite for such an appropriation. Thus, for example, a point of order may be raised in either house objecting to an appropriation in an appropriation act that is not previously authorized by law. An authorization of appropriations may be part of the organic legislation for the agency or program or it may be separate legislation. Oftentimes, the authorization of appropriation may be inferred from an appropriation provided in an appropriation act. The authorization of appropriation may specify the amount of budget authority to be included in the appropriation act or it may authorize the appropriation of "such sums as may be necessary." In some instances, authorizing legislation may contain an appropriation or provide other forms of budget authority, such as contract authority, borrowing authority, or entitlement authority. (*See also* Appropriation Act; Backdoor Authority/Backdoor Spending; Entitlement Authority; Limitation; Point of Order; Reauthorization.)

B

BACKDOOR AUTHORITY/BACKDOOR SPENDING

A colloquial phrase for budget authority provided in laws other than appropriations acts, including contract authority and borrowing authority, as well as entitlement authority and the outlays that result from that budget authority. (*See also* Appropriations *and* Contract Authority *under* Forms of Budget Authority *under* Budget Authority; Authorizing Legislation; Entitlement Authority; Spending Committee.)

BALANCED BUDGET

A budget in which receipts equal outlays. (*See also* Deficit; Surplus.)

BALANCED BUDGET AND EMERGENCY DEFICIT CONTROL ACT OF 1985

Also known as the Deficit Control Act, originally known as Gramm-Rudman-Hollings. Among other changes to the budget process, the law established "maximum deficit amounts" and a sequestration procedure to reduce spending if those targets were exceeded. The Deficit Control Act has been amended and extended several times—most significantly by the Budget Enforcement Act (BEA) of 1990. The sequestration and enforcement mechanisms expired or became ineffective at the end of fiscal year 2002. (*See also* Budget Enforcement Act; Gramm-Rudman-Hollings.)

BALANCED BUDGET AND EMERGENCY DEFICIT CONTROL REAFFIRMATION ACT OF 1987

Amended the Balanced Budget and Emergency Deficit Control Act of 1985 (Gramm-Rudman-Hollings) to extend the date for achieving the goal of a balanced budget until fiscal year 1993, revise sequestration procedures, and require the Director of the Office of Management and Budget (OMB) to determine whether a sequester is necessary. (*See also* Budget and Accounting Act of 1921; Budget Enforcement Act; Gramm-Rudman-Hollings; Sequestration.)

BASELINE

An estimate of spending, revenue, the deficit or surplus, and the public debt expected during a fiscal year under current laws and current policy. The baseline is a benchmark for measuring the budgetary effects of proposed changes in revenues and spending. It assumes that receipts and mandatory spending will continue or expire in the future as required by law and that the future funding for discretionary programs will equal the most recently enacted appropriation, adjusted for inflation. Under the Budget Enforcement Act (BEA), which will expire at the end of fiscal year 2006, the baseline is defined as the projection of current-year levels of new budget authority, outlays, revenues, and the surplus or deficit into the budget year and outyears based on laws enacted through the applicable date. (*See also* Projections.)

CBO Baseline

Projected levels of governmental receipts (revenues), budget authority, and outlays for the budget year and subsequent fiscal years, assuming generally that current policies remain the same, except as directed by law. The baseline is described in the Congressional Budget Office's (CBO) annual report for the House and Senate Budget Committees, *The Budget and Economic Outlook*, which is published in January. The baseline, by law, includes projections for 5 years, but at the request of the Budget Committees, CBO has provided such projections for 10 years. In most years the CBO baseline is revised in conjunction with CBO's analysis of the President's budget, which is usually issued in March, and again during the summer. The "March" baseline is the benchmark for measuring the budgetary effects of proposed legislation under consideration by Congress.

BASES OF BUDGETING

Methods for calculating budget figures. Not all methods are mutually exclusive. For example, the federal budget includes both net and gross figures and reports both obligations and cash or cash equivalent spending. As a general rule, budget receipts and outlays are on a cash or cash equivalent basis; however, interest on public issues of public debt is recorded on an accrual basis. Under credit reform, the subsidy cost of both direct loans and guaranteed loans is included in the budget (i.e., the budget records the net present value of the estimated cash flows of direct loans and loan guarantees as outlays). (*See also* Capital Budget; Direct Loan *and* Guaranteed Loan *under* Federal Credit. For a more detailed presentation of this subject, *see* app. III.)

Accrual Basis

The basis whereby transactions and events are recognized when they occur, regardless of when cash is received or paid. (*See also* Accrual Accounting.)

Budgeting in Relation to Totals

Gross Basis
Budgetary totals from which offsetting collections have not been deducted. In customary use, "gross" refers to the sum or total value of a transaction before reduction by applicable offsets. Under this display, totals include obligations and expenditures from offsetting collections and governmental receipts rather than as offsets to outlays. (*See also* Offsetting Collections *and* Offsetting Receipts *under* Collections.)

Net Basis
The use of budgetary totals from which offsetting collections have been deducted. Under this display, budgetary totals include offsetting collections as offsets to obligations and outlays rather than as receipts. (*See also* Offsetting Collections *under* Collections.)

Cash or Cash Equivalent Basis

The basis whereby receipts are recorded when received and expenditures are recorded when paid, without regard to the accounting period in which the receipts are earned or the costs are incurred. "Cash" generally refers to payment by cash, checks, or electronic funds transfers. "Cash equivalent" refers to the use of an instrument or process that creates a substitute for cash. For example, when the government issues a debt instrument of any kind in satisfaction of claims, the transaction is recorded as simultaneous outlays and borrowing—the outlays when the debt instrument is issued, not when it is redeemed.

Obligations Basis

The basis whereby financial transactions involving the use of funds are recorded in the accounts primarily when goods and services are ordered, regardless of when the resources acquired are to be received or consumed or when cash is received or paid. (*See also* Liability; Obligation.)

BENEFIT-COST ANALYSIS (ECONOMICS TERM)

See under Cost-Benefit Analysis.

BIENNIAL BUDGET

A budget covering a period of 2 years. The federal government has an annual budget, but there have been proposals to shift to a biennial budget. The 2-year period can apply to the budget presented to Congress by the President, to the budget resolution adopted by Congress, or to the frequency and period covered by appropriations acts. The Department of Defense Authorization Act, 1986, Pub. L. No. 99–145, required the Department of Defense to submit 2-year budgets beginning with the budgets for 1988 and 1989. However, to date, appropriations have been made on an annual basis.

BUDGET

A detailed statement of anticipated revenues and expenditures during an accounting period. For the federal government, the term "budget" often refers to the President's budget submission to Congress early each calendar year in accordance with the Budget and Accounting Act of 1921, as amended, and represents proposals for congressional consideration. The President's budget includes requests for budget authority for federal programs and estimates of revenues and outlays for the upcoming fiscal year and, with respect to budget authority requests in some cases, for future fiscal years. By law, elements of the budget, such as the estimates for the legislative branch and the judiciary, must be included without review by the Office of Management and Budget (OMB) or approval by the President. In the context of individual federal agencies and their programs, the term "budget" also may be used to refer to their budget submissions or, in response to Congress passing laws providing budget authority, the agencies' plans for spending the funds they were provided. (*See also* President's Budget; app. I.)

BUDGET ACT

The common name of the Congressional Budget and Impoundment Control Act of 1974. (*See under* Congressional Budget and Impoundment Control Act of 1974.)

BUDGET ACTIVITY

A specific and distinguishable line of work performed by a governmental unit to discharge a function or subfunction for which the governmental unit is responsible. Activities within most accounts identify the purposes, projects, or types of activities financed. For example, food inspection is an activity performed in the discharge of the health function. A budget activity is presented in the Program by Activities section in the Program and Financing Schedule for each account in the President's budget. (*See also* Functional Classification; for a partial distinction, *see* Program, Project, or Activity.)

BUDGET AMENDMENT

A revision to a pending budget request that the President submits to Congress before Congress completes appropriations action.

BUDGET AND ACCOUNTING ACT OF 1921

Enhanced budgetary efficiency and aided in the performance of constitutional checks and balances through the budget process. It required the President to submit a national budget each year and restricted the authority of the agencies to present their own proposals. (See 31 U.S.C. §§ 1104, 1105.) With this centralization of authority for the formulation of the executive branch budget in the President and the newly established Bureau of the Budget (now the Office of Management and Budget (OMB)), Congress also took steps to strengthen its oversight of fiscal matters by establishing the General Accounting Office, renamed the Government Accountability Office (GAO) in 2004.

BUDGET AUTHORITY

Authority provided by federal law to enter into financial obligations that will result in immediate or future outlays involving federal government funds. The basic forms of budget authority include (1) appropriations, (2) borrowing authority, (3) contract authority, and (4) authority to obligate and expend offsetting receipts and collections. Budget authority includes the credit subsidy cost for direct loan and loan guarantee programs, but does not include the underlying authority to insure or guarantee the repayment of indebtedness incurred by another person or government.

Budget authority may be classified by its duration (1-year, multiple-year, or no-year), by the timing provided in the legislation (current or permanent), by the manner of determining the amount available (definite or indefinite), or by its availability for new obligations. (*See also* Current Level Estimate; Credit Subsidy Cost, Direct Loan, *and* Guaranteed Loan *under* Federal Credit; Offsetting Collections *under* Collections.)

Forms of Budget Authority

Appropriations

Budget authority to incur obligations and to make payments from the Treasury for specified purposes. An appropriation act is the most common means of providing appropriations; however, authorizing and other legislation itself may provide appropriations. (*See also* Backdoor Authority/Backdoor Spending.)

Appropriations do not represent cash actually set aside in the Treasury for purposes specified in the appropriation act; they represent amounts that agencies may obligate during the period of time specified in the respective appropriation acts. An appropriation may make funds available from the general fund, special funds, or trust funds. Certain types of appropriations are not counted as budget authority because they do not provide authority to incur obligations. Among these are appropriations to liquidate contract authority (legislation to provide funds to pay obligations incurred against contract authority), to redeem outstanding debt (legislation to provide funds for debt retirement), and to refund receipts. Sometimes appropriations are contingent upon the occurrence of some other action specified in the appropriation law, such as the enactment of a subsequent authorization or the fulfillment of some action by the executive branch. (*See also* Appropriation

Act; Discretionary; Expired Budget Authority *under* Availability for New Obligations *under* Budget Authority; Mandatory.)

Borrowing Authority

Budget authority enacted to permit an agency to borrow money and then to obligate against amounts borrowed. It may be definite or indefinite in nature. Usually the funds are borrowed from the Treasury, but in a few cases agencies borrow directly from the public. (*See also* Debt, Federal.)

Contract Authority

Budget authority that permits an agency to incur obligations in advance of appropriations, including collections sufficient to liquidate the obligation or receipts. Contract authority is unfunded, and a subsequent appropriation or offsetting collection is needed to liquidate the obligations. The Food and Forage Act (41 U.S.C. § 11) and the Price Anderson Act (42 U.S.C. § 2210) are examples of such authority. (*See also* Backdoor Authority/Backdoor Spending.)

Offsetting Receipts and Collections

A form of budget authority that permits agencies to obligate and expend the proceeds of offsetting receipts and collections. The Congressional Budget Act of 1974, as amended by the Budget Enforcement Act (BEA) of 1990, defines offsetting receipts and collections as negative budget authority and the reductions to it as positive budget authority. In the President's budget, the Office of Management and Budget (OMB) reports offsetting receipts as appropriations.

Duration

One-Year Authority

Budget authority available for obligation only during a specific fiscal year that expires at the end of that fiscal year. It is also known as "fiscal year" or "annual" budget authority.

Multiple-Year Authority (Multiyear)

Budget authority available for a fixed period of time in excess of 1 fiscal year. This authority generally takes the form of 2-year, 3-year, and so forth, availability but may cover periods that do not coincide with the start or end of a fiscal year. For example, the authority may be available from July 1 of one fiscal year through September 30 of the following fiscal year, a period of 15 months. This latter type of multiple-year authority is sometimes referred to as "forward funding." (For a distinction, *see* Advance Appropriation; Advance Funding. *See also* Full Funding.)

No-Year Authority

Budget authority that remains available for obligation for an indefinite period of time. A no-year appropriation is usually identified by language such as "to remain available until expended."

Reappropriation

Legislation permitting an agency to obligate, whether for the same or different purposes, all or part of the unobligated portion of budget authority that has expired or would otherwise expire if not reappropriated. In the President's budget, reappropriations of expired balances are counted as new budget authority or balance transfers depending on the year for which the amounts are reappropriated.

Timing of Legislative Action

Current Authority

Budget authority made available by Congress for the fiscal year or years during which the funds are available for obligation.

Permanent Authority

Budget authority that is available as the result of previously enacted legislation and is available without further legislative action. For example, authority to retain and use offsetting receipts tends to be permanent authority. Such budget authority can be the result of substantive legislation or appropriation acts.

Determination of Amount

Definite Authority

Budget authority that is stated as a specified sum at the time the authority is enacted. This type of authority, whether in an appropriation act or other law, includes authority stated as "not to exceed" a specified amount.

Indefinite Authority

Budget authority that, at time of enactment, is for an unspecified amount. Indefinite budget authority may be appropriated as all or part of the amount of proceeds from the sale of financial assets, the amount necessary to cover obligations associated with payments, the receipts from specified sources—the exact amount of which is determinable only at some future date—or it may be appropriated as "such sums as may be necessary" for a given purpose.

Availability for New Obligations

Expired Budget Authority

Budget authority that is no longer available to incur new obligations but is available for an additional 5 fiscal years for disbursement of obligations properly incurred during the budget authority's period of availability. Unobligated balances of expired budget authority remain available for 5 years to cover legitimate obligation adjustments or for obligations properly incurred during the budget authority's period of availability that the agency failed to record. (See 31 U.S.C. §§ 1552(a), 1553(a).) (*See also* Expired Account; Unobligated Balance *under* Obligational Authority; Warrant.)

Unexpired Budget Authority

Budget authority that is available for incurring new obligations.

BUDGET ENFORCEMENT ACT (BEA)

First enacted as Title XIII of the Omnibus Budget Reconciliation Act of 1990. BEA amended the Balanced Budget and Emergency Deficit Control Act of 1985 and related amendments (Gramm-Rudman-Hollings) and the Congressional Budget and Impoundment Control Act of 1974. BEA modified procedures and definitions for sequestration and deficit reduction, reformed budgetary credit accounting, maintained the off-budget status of the Old-Age and Survivors Insurance and Disability Insurance Trust Funds, and removed Social Security trust fund receipts and outlays from deficit and sequestration calculations through fiscal year 1995. Public Law 103–66 (1993) extended the discretionary spending limits, pay-as-you-go (PAYGO) rules, and sequestration procedures through fiscal year 1998. The BEA of 1997, enacted as part of the Balanced Budget Act of 1997, further extended these budget enforcement mechanisms through fiscal year 2002. The BEA of 1997 also added new categories of discretionary spending and made technical and conforming changes to correct drafting errors in the BEA of 1990.

The sequestration and enforcement mechanisms of the Balanced Budget and Emergency Deficit Control Act, as amended by BEA, expired or became ineffective, at the end of fiscal year 2002. (All BEA-specific terms are defined in *A Glossary of Terms Used in the Federal Budget Process: Exposure Draft*, January 1993, GAO/AFMD-2.1.1.) (*See also* Credit Reform; Direct Spending; Gramm-Rudman-Hollings; Mandatory; Off-Budget.)

BUDGET ESTIMATES

Estimates of budget authority, outlays, receipts, budget amendments, supplemental requests from the President, or other budget measures that cover the current, budget, and future years, as reflected in the President's budget and budget updates. (*See also* Budget Update.)

BUDGET OF THE U.S. GOVERNMENT

See under President's Budget.

BUDGET RECEIPTS

See Governmental Receipts *under* Collections.

BUDGET RESOLUTION

See under Concurrent Resolution on the Budget.

BUDGET UPDATE

A revised estimate of budget authority, receipts, and outlays issued subsequent to the issuance of the President's budget. The President is required by provisions of the Congressional Budget and Impoundment Control Act of 1974 (see provisions of 31 U.S.C. §§ 1105(d), 1106) to transmit such statements to Congress by July 15 of each year; however, the President may also submit budget updates at other times during the fiscal year. (*See also* Budget Estimates.)

BUDGET YEAR

See under Fiscal Year.

BUDGETARY ACCOUNTING

See under Obligational Accounting.

BUDGETARY ACCOUNTS

See under Standard General Ledger (SGL) Chart of Accounts.

BUDGETARY RESERVES

Portions of budgetary resources set aside (withheld through apportionment) by the Office of Management and Budget (OMB) by authority of the Antideficiency Act (31 U.S.C. § 1512) solely to provide for contingencies or to effect savings. Such savings are made possible through changes in requirements or through greater efficiency of operations.

Budgetary resources may also be set aside if specifically provided for by particular appropriation acts or other laws.

Except as specifically provided by law, no reserves shall be established other than as authorized under the Antideficiency Act (31 U.S.C. § 1512). Reserves established are reported to Congress in accordance with provisions of the Impoundment Control Act of 1974 (2 U.S.C. §§ 681–688). (*See also* Antideficiency Act; Apportionment; Deferral of Budget Authority; Rescission.)

BUDGETARY RESOURCES

An amount available to enter into new obligations and to liquidate them. Budgetary resources are made up of new budget authority (including direct spending authority provided in existing statute and obligation limitations) and unobligated balances of budget authority provided in previous years. (*See also* Budget Authority.)

BYRD RULE

A rule of the Senate that allows a senator to strike extraneous material in, or proposed to be in, reconciliation legislation or the related conference report. The rule defines six provisions that are "extraneous," including a provision that does not produce a change in outlays or revenues and a provision that produces changes in outlays or revenues that are merely incidental to the nonbudgetary components of the provision. The Byrd Rule was first enacted as section 20001 of the Consolidated Omnibus Budget Reconciliation Act of 1985 and later transferred in 1990 to section 313 of the Congressional Budget Act (2 U.S.C. § 644). The rule is named after its primary sponsor, Senator Robert C. Byrd. (*See also* Reconciliation; Reconciliation Bill; Reconciliation Instruction; Reconciliation Resolution.)

C

CAPITAL

Has different meanings depending on the context in which it is used.

Physical capital is land and the stock of products set aside to support future production and consumption. In the National Income and Product Accounts, private capital consists of business inventories, producers' durable equipment, and residential and nonresidential structures. (*See* National Income and Product Accounts.) *Financial capital* is funds raised by governments, individuals, or businesses by incurring liabilities such as bonds, mortgages, or stock certificates. *Human capital* is the education, training, work experience, and other attributes that enhance the ability of the labor force to produce goods and services.

Capital assets are land, structures, equipment, intellectual property (e.g., software), and information technology (including information technology service contracts) that are used by the federal government and have an estimated useful life of 2 years or more. Capital assets may be acquired in different ways: through purchase, construction, or manufacturing; through a lease-purchase or other capital lease (regardless of whether title has passed to the federal government); through an operating lease for an asset with an estimated useful life of 2 years or more; or through exchange.

Capital assets may or may not be recorded in an entity's balance sheet under federal accounting standards. Capital assets do not include grants to state and local governments or other entities for acquiring capital assets (such as National Science Foundation grants to universities or Department of Transportation grants to Amtrak), intangible assets (such as the knowledge resulting from research and development), or the human capital resulting from education and training. For more on capital assets, consult the *Capital Programming Guide* (June 1997), a supplement to OMB Circular No. A-11.

CAPITAL BUDGET

A budget that segregates capital investments from the operating budget's expenditures. In such a budget, the capital investments that are excluded from the operating budget do not count toward calculating the operating budget's surplus or deficit at the time the investment is made. States that use capital budgets usually include only part of their capital expenditures in that budget and normally finance the capital investment from borrowing and then charge amortization (interest and debt repayment) to the operating budget.

CAPITAL LEASE

A lease other than a lease-purchase that transfers substantially all the benefits and risks of ownership to the lessee and does not meet the criteria of an operating lease. (*See also* Operating Lease.)

CASH ACCOUNTING

A system of accounting in which revenues are recorded when cash is actually received and expenses are recorded when payment is made without regard to the accounting period in which the revenues were earned or costs were incurred. (*See also* Accrual Accounting; app. III.)

CHAIN PRICE INDEXES (ECONOMICS TERM)

Index calculated by linking (chaining) of price indexes based on changing weights to create a time series. Chain-type indexes are used in the Bureau of Economic Analysis National Income and Product Accounts (NIPA). (*See also* Chained Dollars; Real Dollar.)

CHAINED DOLLARS (ECONOMICS TERM)

Dollar values calculated by taking the current dollar level of a series in the base period (or period from which the weights for a measurement series are derived) and multiplying it by the change in the chain quantity index number for the series (calculated using chained weights) since the base period. Chained-dollar estimates correctly show growth rates for a series, but the summed components do not equal the aggregate in periods other than the period from which the weights for a measurement series are derived. (*See also* Chain Price Indexes; Real Dollar.)

CLOSED (CANCELED) ACCOUNT

An appropriation account whose balance has been canceled. Once balances are canceled, the amounts are not available for obligation or expenditure for any purpose. An account available for a definite period (fixed appropriation account) is canceled 5 fiscal years after the period of availability for obligation ends. An account available for an indefinite period (no-year account) is canceled if (1) the head of the agency concerned or the President determines that the purposes for which the appropriation was made have been carried out and (2) no disbursement has been made against the appropriation for 2 consecutive fiscal years. (*See also* Expired Account; Obligational Authority.)

COLLECTIONS

Amounts received by the federal government during the fiscal year. Collections are classified into three major categories: (1) governmental receipts (also called budget receipts or federal receipts), (2) offsetting collections, and (3) offsetting receipts.

Governmental receipts result from the exercise of the government's sovereign powers. Offsetting collections and receipts result from businesslike transactions with the public or transactions between appropriated activities. Offsetting collections and offsetting receipts are recorded as offsets to spending. They are offsetting collections when the collections are authorized by law to be credited to expenditure accounts. Otherwise, they are deposited in receipt accounts and called offsetting receipts.

For further discussion, see "Federal Receipts and Collections" in the *Analytical Perspectives* of the President's budget. (*See also* Account in the President's Budget; Off-Budget; On-Budget; Revenue.)

Governmental Receipts

Collections from the public based on the government's exercise of its sovereign powers, including individual and corporate income taxes and social insurance taxes, excise taxes, duties, court fines, compulsory licenses, and deposits of earnings by the Federal Reserve System. Gifts and contributions (as distinguished from payments for services or cost-sharing deposits by state and local governments) are also counted as governmental receipts. Total governmental receipts include those specifically designated as off-budget by provisions of law. Total governmental receipts are compared with total outlays in calculating the budget surplus or deficit. (*See also*

Federal Fund Accounts *under* Account in the President's Budget; Gross Basis *and* Net Basis *under* Budgeting in Relation to Totals *under* Bases of Budgeting; Off-Budget; On-Budget.)

Offsetting Collections

Collections authorized by law to be credited to appropriation or fund expenditure accounts. They result from (1) businesslike transactions or market-oriented activities with the public, (2) intragovernmental transfers, and (3) collections from the public that are governmental in nature but required by law to be classified as offsetting. Collections resulting from businesslike transactions with the public and other government accounts are also known as reimbursements.

Laws authorizing offsetting collections make them available for obligation to meet the account's purpose without further legislative action. However, it is not uncommon for annual appropriation acts to include limitations on the obligations to be financed by these collections. The authority to obligate and spend offsetting collections is a form of budget authority. The Congressional Budget Act of 1974, as amended by the Budget Enforcement Act (BEA) of 1990, defines offsetting collections as negative budget authority and the reductions to it as positive budget authority.

Offsetting collections include reimbursements, transfers between federal and trust fund accounts, offsetting governmental collections, and refunds.

Reimbursements

When authorized by law, amounts collected for materials or services furnished to the public or other government accounts. (For accounting purposes, earned reimbursements are also known as revenues.) These offsetting collections are netted against gross outlays in determining net outlays from such appropriations. (*See also* Unfilled Customer Orders.)

Transfers Between Federal and Trust Fund Accounts

Transfers of resources between federal and trust fund accounts are treated as expenditure transfers regardless of the nature of the transaction. The receiving account reports offsetting collections from federal sources (for offsetting collections) or intragovernmental receipts (for offsetting receipts).

Offsetting Governmental Collections

A term used by the Office of Management and Budget (OMB) to designate offsetting collections from nonfederal sources that are governmental in nature but are required by law to be credited to expenditure accounts.

Refunds

Payments returned to the government that were made in error. They are credited to the appropriation originally charged. (*See also* Offsetting Collections *under* Collections.)

Offsetting Receipts

Collections that are offset against gross outlays but are not authorized to be credited to expenditure accounts. Offsetting receipts are deposited in receipt accounts. Like offsetting collections, they result from (1) businesslike transactions or market-oriented activities with the public, (2) intragovernmental transfers, and (3) collections from the public that are governmental in nature but required by law to be classified as offsetting receipts.

Offsetting receipts are offsets to gross budget authority and outlays, usually at the agency or subfunction level, but some are undistributed and are offsets to budget authority and outlays in the aggregate. (*See also* Undistributed Offsetting Receipts.)

Unlike offsetting collections, offsetting receipts cannot be used without being appropriated. Trust fund offsetting receipts are permanently appropriated and, therefore, can be used without subsequent annual appropriation legislation. (*See* Permanent Authority *under* Timing of Legislative Action *under* Budget Authority; Trust Fund Receipt Account *under* Trust Fund Accounts *under* Account in the President's Budget.) The Congressional Budget Act of 1974, as amended by the Budget Enforcement Act (BEA) of 1990, defines offsetting receipts and collections as negative budget authority and the reductions to it as positive budget authority. (*See also* Earmarking; Reimbursement.)

Proprietary Receipts from the Public

Collections from outside the government that are deposited in receipt accounts that arise as a result of the government's business-type or market-oriented activities. Among these are interest received, proceeds from the sale of property and products, charges for nonregulatory services, and rents and royalties. Such collections may be credited to general fund, special fund, or trust fund receipt accounts and are offset against budget authority and outlays. In most cases, such offsets are by agency and by subfunction, but some proprietary receipts are deducted from total budget authority and outlays for the government as a whole. An example of the latter is rents and royalties on the Outer Continental Shelf. (*See* Subfunction 953 in app. IV. *See also* Earmarking.

Intragovernmental Transfers

Collections from other federal government accounts, often as payment for goods or services provided. Most offsetting receipts from intragovernmental transfers are offset against budget authority and outlays of the agency or subfunction that produced the goods or services. However, two intragovernmental transfers are classified as undistributed offsetting receipts: (1) agency payments as employers into employee retirement trust funds and (2) interest received by trust funds. These offsetting receipts appear as offsets to budget authority and outlays for the government as a whole, rather than at the agency level.

Intragovernmental transfers may be (1) intrabudgetary (on-budget), (2) off-budget, or (3) transfers between on-budget and off-budget accounts. Intrabudgetary transfers are further subdivided into three categories: (1) interfund transfers, where the payment is from one fund group, either federal or trust, to a receipt account in the other fund group; (2) federal intrafund transfers, where the payment and receipt both occur within the federal fund group; and (3) trust intrafund transfers, where the payment and receipt both occur within the trust fund group.

Offsetting Governmental Receipts

A term used by the Office of Management and Budget (OMB) to designate receipts that are governmental in nature (e.g., tax receipts, regulatory fees, and compulsory user charges) but are required by law to be classified as offsetting.

COMBINED STATEMENT OF RECEIPTS, OUTLAYS, AND BALANCES OF THE UNITED STATES GOVERNMENT

The Department of the Treasury's annual accounting of the (1) unified budget receipts activities of the federal government, which should be consistent with the aggregated custodial nonexchange revenues (before net accrual adjustment) reported in federal agencies' statements of custodial activity, and (2) unified budget outlays activities of the federal government, which should be consistent with net outlays reported in federal agencies' statements of budgetary resources. This report also provides a summary accounting of agencies' budget activities: appropriations, borrowings and investments, outlays, and balances based on the agencies' budget execution reports. (*See also* Monthly Treasury Statement.)

COMMITMENT

An administrative reservation of allotted funds, or of other funds, in anticipation of their obligation. For federal proprietary accounting, a commitment may also manifest an intent to expend assets (e.g., to provide government social insurance benefits). See Statement of Federal Financial Accounting Standards (SFFAS) No. 25,
Basis for Conclusions, para. 8, and SFFAS No. 17, *Basis for Conclusions*, paras. 65 and 94. (*See also* Allotment; Loan Guarantee Commitment *under* Federal Credit; Obligation.)

COMMITTEE ALLOCATION

The distribution of total proposed new budget authority and outlays, as set forth in the concurrent resolution on the budget, among the congressional committees according to their jurisdictions. The allocations are set forth in the joint explanatory statement of managers included in the conference report on the congressional budget resolution. House and Senate committees receive allocations of total new budget authority and total outlays. House committees also receive allocations of total entitlement authority, and Senate committees also receive allocations of Social Security outlays. Allocations are committee specific, but not program specific.

Under section 302(a) of the Congressional Budget and Impoundment Control Act of 1974 (2 U.S.C. § 633(a)), committee allocations are limits, not simply recommendations. (*See also* Allocation; Concurrent Resolution on the Budget; Entitlement Authority.)

Comparative Statement of New Budget Authority

A table accompanying a regular or supplemental appropriations act in the report of the House or Senate Appropriations Committee. It compares the appropriation recommended for each account in that act with the amount requested by the President in the budget submission and the amount enacted in the preceding fiscal year. In some cases, such as when a continuing appropriations act is considered, the statement may be inserted into the *Congressional Record.*

CONCURRENT RESOLUTION ON THE BUDGET

A concurrent resolution adopted by both houses of Congress as part of the annual budget and appropriations process, setting forth an overall budget plan for Congress against which individual appropriations bills, other appropriations, and revenue measures are to be evaluated. As a plan for Congress, the resolution is not presented to the President for signature and does not have the force of law. Pursuant to section 301 of the Congressional Budget Act, as amended (2 U.S.C. § 632), the resolution is expected to establish, for at least 5 fiscal years beginning on October 1 of the year of the resolution, appropriate levels for the following:

- totals of new budget authority and outlays,
- total federal revenues,
- the surplus or deficit in the budget,
- new budget authority and outlays for each major functional category,
- the public debt, and
- outlays and revenues for Social Security insurance programs.

The concurrent resolution generally contains budget levels for the 5 fiscal years and may contain reconciliation instructions to specified committees. The concurrent resolution most recently adopted may be revised or affirmed before the end of the year to which it applies, as provided in section 304 of the Congressional Budget Act, as amended (2 U.S.C. § 635). (*See also* Congressional Budget and Impoundment Control Act of 1974.)

CONGRESSIONAL BUDGET

The Concurrent Resolution on the Budget is oftentimes referred to as the Congressional Budget. (*See* Concurrent Resolution on the Budget.)

CONGRESSIONAL BUDGET ACT

Titles I–IX of the Congressional Budget and Impoundment Control Act of 1974, as amended (2 U.S.C. §§ 601–661), are commonly referred to as the Congressional Budget Act. (*See also* Congressional Budget and Impoundment Control Act of 1974. For an overview of the federal budget process, *see* app. I.)

CONGRESSIONAL BUDGET AND IMPOUNDMENT CONTROL ACT OF 1974

Established a process through which Congress could systematically consider the total spending policy of the United States and determine priorities for allocating budgetary resources. The process calls for procedures for coordinating congressional revenue and spending decisions made in separate tax, appropriations, and legislative measures. It established the House and Senate Budget Committees, the Congressional Budget Office (CBO), and the procedures for congressional review of impoundments in the form of rescissions and deferrals proposed by the President. (*See also* Budget Enforcement Act; Deferral of Budget Authority; Gramm-Rudman-Hollings; Impoundment; Rescission.)

CONSOLIDATED BUDGET

See under Unified Budget.

CONSOLIDATED FINANCIAL STATEMENT

The financial statements of a parent and its subsidiary or component entities, presented as if the group were a single entity. In the U.S. government, there is a consolidated financial statement for the federal government that encompasses the executive, legislative, and judicial branches as well as consolidated statements for agencies that encompass all their offices, bureaus, and activities.

CONSTANT DOLLARS (ECONOMICS TERM)

See under Real Dollar.

CONSUMER PRICE INDEX (CPI) (ECONOMICS TERM)

A measure of the average change over time in the prices paid by urban consumers for a market basket of consumer goods and services commonly referred to as "inflation." Measures for two population groups are currently published, CPI-U and CPI-W. CPI-U is based on a market basket determined by expenditure patterns of all urban households, while the market basket for CPI-W is determined by expenditure patterns of only urban wage-earner and clerical-worker families. The urban wage-earner and clerical-worker population consists of clerical workers, sales workers, craft workers, operatives, service workers, and laborers. Both indexes are published monthly by the Bureau of Labor Statistics. The CPI is used to adjust for inflation, the income payments of Social Security beneficiaries, and payments made by other programs. In addition, the CPI is used to adjust certain amounts defined by the tax code, such as personal exemptions and the tax brackets.

CONTINGENT LIABILITY

An existing condition, situation, or set of circumstances that poses the possibility of a loss to an agency that will ultimately be resolved when one or more events occur or fail to occur. Contingent liabilities may lead to outlays. Contingent liabilities may arise, for example, with respect to unadjudicated claims, assessments, loan guarantee programs, and federal insurance programs. Contingent liabilities are normally not covered by budget authority in advance. However, credit reform changed the normal budgetary treatment of loans and loan guarantees by establishing that for most programs, loan guarantee commitments cannot be made unless Congress has made appropriations of budget authority to cover the credit subsidy cost in advance in annual appropriations acts. (*See also* Credit Subsidy Cost *under* Federal Credit; Liability.)

CONTINUING APPROPRIATION/CONTINUING RESOLUTION (OFTEN REFERRED TO SIMPLY AS "CR")

An appropriation act that provides budget authority for federal agencies, specific activities, or both to continue in operation when Congress and the President have not completed action on the regular appropriation acts by the beginning of the fiscal year. Enacted in the form of a joint resolution, a continuing resolution is passed by both houses of Congress and signed into law by the President. A continuing resolution may be enacted for the full year, up to a specified date, or until regular appropriations are enacted. A continuing resolution usually specifies a maximum rate at which the obligations may be incurred based on levels specified in the resolution. For example, the resolution may state that obligations may not exceed the current rate or must be the lower of the amounts provided in the appropriation bills passed in the House or Senate. If enacted to cover the entire fiscal year, the resolution will usually specify amounts provided for each appropriation account. (*See also* Appropriation Act; Current Rate; Joint Resolution; Seasonal Rate; Supplemental Appropriation.)

COST

The price or cash value of the resources used to produce a program, project, or activity. This term is used in many different contexts. When used in connection with federal credit programs, the term means the estimated long-term cost to the government of a direct loan or loan guarantee, calculated on a net present value basis over the life of the loan, excluding administrative costs and any incidental effects on governmental receipts or outlays. (*See also* Credit Subsidy Cost *under* Federal Credit; Expense.)

For federal proprietary accounting, the monetary value of resources used or sacrificed or the liabilities incurred to achieve an objective.

In economic terms, it is a measure of what must be given up in order to obtain something, whether by purchase, exchange, or production. Economists generally use the concept of opportunity cost, which is the value of all of the things that must be forgone or given up in obtaining something. The opportunity cost measure may, but will not always, equal the money outlays used to measure accounting costs. Economists sometimes distinguish between the private costs of a good or activity to the consumer or producer and the social costs imposed on the community as a whole.

COST-BENEFIT ANALYSIS (ECONOMICS TERM)

An analytic technique that compares the costs and benefits of investments, programs, or policy actions in order to determine which alternative or alternatives maximize net benefits (economic efficiency). Cost-benefit analysis attempts to consider all costs and benefits to whomever they accrue, regardless of whether they are reflected in market transactions. The costs and benefits included depend upon the scope of the analysis, although the standard federal analysis is national in scope. Net benefits of an alternative are determined by subtracting the present value of costs from the present value of benefits. (*See also* Present Value.)

COST ESTIMATES

Under the Congressional Budget Act of 1974, estimates of the impact legislation under consideration by Congress would have on the federal budget if the legislation became law. Cost estimates are provided by the Congressional Budget Office (CBO) on all legislation of a public character reported by a congressional committee and are, typically, published in the report accompanying that legislation.

COUNTERCYCLICAL POLICY (ECONOMICS TERM)

Policy aimed at reducing the size and duration of swings in economic activity in order to keep economic growth closer to a pace consistent with low inflation and high employment. It includes monetary and fiscal policies affecting the level of interest rates, money supply, taxes, and government spending.

CREDIT, CREDIT REFORM

See under Federal Credit.

CURRENT DOLLAR (ECONOMICS TERM)

"In current dollars" means valued in the prices of the current year. The current dollar value of a good or service is its value in terms of prices current at the time the good or service is acquired or sold.

CURRENT LEVEL ESTIMATE

An estimate of the amounts of new budget authority, outlays, and revenues for a full fiscal year, based upon enacted law. Current level estimates used by Congress do not take into account the potential effects of pending legislation. Current level estimates include a tabulation comparing estimates with the aggregates approved in the most recent budget resolution, and they are consistent with the technical and economic assumptions in that resolution. This means that the current level is not only compared to the resolution, but the current level estimate's framework is consistent with the resolution. Section 308(b) of the Congressional Budget and Impoundment Control Act of 1974, as amended (2 U.S.C. § 639(b)), requires the House and Senate Budget Committees to make this tabulation at least once a month. The Congressional Budget Office (CBO) assists these committees by regularly submitting reports of the budgetary impact of congressional actions. (*See also* Budget Authority; Committee Allocation; Congressional Budget Act; Scorekeeping.)

CURRENT RATE

Used in a continuing resolution, the total amount of budget authority that was available for obligation for an activity during the fiscal year immediately prior to the one for which the continuing resolution is enacted. Congress often uses the "current rate" as part of a formula to indicate a level of spending that it desires for a program for the duration of the continuing resolution. The current rate does not allow agencies to fund new initiatives, programs, or both requested for the current year unless Congress specifically authorizes them to be funded. (*See also* Continuing Appropriation/ Continuing Resolution; Seasonal Rate.)

CURRENT SERVICES ESTIMATES

Estimates submitted by the President of the levels of budget authority and outlays for the ensuing fiscal year based on the continuation of existing levels of service. These estimates reflect the anticipated costs of continuing federal programs and activities at present levels without policy changes. Such estimates ignore all new presidential or congressional initiatives, including reductions or increases that are not yet law.

With the proposed budget each year, the President must transmit current services estimates and the economic assumptions upon which they are based. Updated current services estimates are also included in the *Mid-Session Review* of the President's budget, but are not identified by that title and are confined to those programs that are essentially automatic (that is, they exclude programs controlled through annual appropriations). The current services data in the *Mid-Session Review* are identified as being for "mandatory and related programs under current law."

The Congressional Budget Office (CBO) also prepares similar estimates. For a more detailed discussion of this term, see "Current Services Estimates" in the *Analytical Perspectives* of the President's budget. (*See also* Baseline; Multiyear Budget Planning.)

CURRENT YEAR

See under Fiscal Year.

CYCLICAL SURPLUS/DEFICIT (ECONOMICS TERM)

The part of the federal budget surplus or deficit that results from cyclical factors rather than from underlying fiscal policy. This cyclical component reflects the way in which the surplus or deficit automatically increases or decreases during economic booms or recessions.

CYCLICALLY ADJUSTED SURPLUS OR DEFICIT (ECONOMICS TERM)

The portion of surplus or deficit remaining after the impact of the business cycle has been removed.

D

DAILY TREASURY STATEMENT (DTS)

See under Monthly Treasury Statement.

DEBT, FEDERAL

Generally, the amount borrowed by the government from the public or from government accounts. Four ways that federal debt may be categorized for reporting purposes are (1) gross federal debt, (2) debt held by the public, (3) debt held by government accounts, and (4) debt subject to statutory debt limit. For a fuller discussion of federal debt, see *Federal Debt: Answers to Frequently Asked Questions. An Update* (GAO-04-485SP). (*See also* Borrowing Authority *under* Forms of Budget Authority *under* Budget Authority; Federal Financing Bank; Means of Financing.)

Buyback

In the context of federal debt, the Department of the Treasury's purchases of marketable Treasury securities from the public prior to their maturity through competitive redemption processes (as opposed to redemptions prior to maturity under call provisions) are often referred to as "debt buybacks." The budget records buyback premiums and discounts as means of financing a surplus or deficit, rather than as outlays or offsetting collections or receipts. The buyback premium or discount is the difference between the reacquisition price of a security and its book value. (*See also* Means of Financing.)

Debt Held by Government Accounts (Intragovernmental Debt)

Federal debt owed by the federal government to itself. Most of this debt is held by trust funds, such as Social Security and Medicare. The Office of Management and Budget (OMB) contrasts it to debt held by the public by noting that it is not a current transaction of the government with the public; it is not financed by private saving and thus does not compete with the private sector for available funds in the credit market; and it does not represent an obligation to make payments to the public.

Debt Held by the Public

That portion of the gross federal debt held outside of the federal government. This includes any federal debt held by individuals, corporations, state or local governments, the Federal Reserve System, and foreign governments and central banks. Debt held by government accounts (intragovernmental debt) is excluded from debt held by the public. Debt held by the public is not the same as public debt or Treasury debt.

Debt Subject to Statutory Debt Limit

Debt guaranteed as to principal and interest by the United States.

As defined by section 3101 of title 31 of the *United States Code*, the debt subject to the statutory debt limit includes debt issued under chapter 31 of that title. This includes Treasury debt except the securities issued by the Federal Financing Bank (FFB) under authority of section 9(a) of the Federal Financing Bank Act of 1973 (12 U.S.C. § 2888(a)) upon which there is a separate limit of $15 billion, and a small amount of agency debt. Agency debt that by law is not guaranteed as to principal and interest by the United States—for example, the Tennessee Valley Authority (TVA) (under authority of section 15d of the TVA Act of 1933, 16 U.S.C. § 831n-4) and the United States Postal Service (under authority of 39 U.S.C. § 2005(a))—is not subject to the ceiling imposed by section 3101, but is usually subject to its own ceiling.

Gross Federal Debt

The total amount of federal government debt comprising debt securities issued by the Department of the Treasury (including securities issued by the Federal Financing Bank (FFB) under section 9(a) of the Federal Financing Bank Act of 1973 (12 U.S.C. § 2888(a)) and other government agencies. Gross federal debt is the sum of debt held by the public and debt held by government accounts (intragovernmental debt).

Treasury Debt/Public Debt

That portion of the gross federal debt issued by the Department of the Treasury to the public or to government accounts (including securities issued by the Federal Financing Bank (FFB) under section 9(a) of the Federal Financing Bank Act of 1973 (12 U.S.C. § 2888(a)). (*See also* Debt Held by Government Accounts *under* Debt, Federal.)

Agency Debt

That portion of the gross federal debt incurred when a federal agency other than the Department of the Treasury (Treasury) is authorized by law to issue debt securities directly to the public or to another government account. While an agency may have authority to borrow directly from the public, agencies usually borrow from Treasury's Federal Financing Bank (FFB). Since Treasury borrowing required to obtain the money to lend to the agency through FFB is already part of the gross federal debt, to avoid double counting, agency borrowing from FFB is not included in the gross federal debt. In addition, federal fund advances from Treasury to trust funds are not included in the gross federal debt to avoid double counting. Debt of government-sponsored, privately owned enterprises, such as the Federal National Mortgage Association, is not included in the federal debt.

Statutory Debt Limit

The ceiling on the amount of most Treasury and agency debt established by section 3101 of title 31 of the *United States Code*, sometimes referred to as the public debt ceiling or the public debt limit.

DEBT SERVICE

Payment of interest on, and repayment of principal on, borrowed funds. The term may also be used to refer to payment of interest alone. (*See also* Means of Financing.) As used in the Congressional Budget Office's (CBO) *Budget and Economic Outlook*, debt service refers to a change in interest payments resulting from a change in estimates of the surplus or the deficit.

DEEMING RESOLUTION

An informal term that refers to a resolution or bill passed by one or both houses of Congress that in the absence of a concurrent resolution, serves for the chamber passing it as an annual budget resolution for purposes of establishing enforceable budget levels for a budget cycle. The Congressional Budget and Impoundment Control Act of 1974 requires the adoption each year of a concurrent resolution on the budget. (*See* Concurrent Resolution on the Budget.)

At a minimum, deeming resolutions provide new spending allocations to the appropriations committees, but they also may set new aggregate budget levels, provide revised spending allocations to other House and Senate committees, or provide for other related purposes. A deeming resolution may even declare that a budget resolution (in its entirety), passed earlier in the session by one house is deemed to have the force and effect as if adopted by both houses.

Deferral of Budget Authority

Temporary withholding or delaying of the obligation or expenditure of budget authority or any other type of executive action, which effectively precludes the obligation or expenditure of budget authority. A deferral is one type of impoundment. Under the Impoundment Control Act of 1974 (2 U.S.C. § 684), budget authority may only be deferred to provide for contingencies, to achieve savings or greater efficiency in the operations of the government, or as otherwise specifically provided by law. Budget authority may not be deferred for policy or any other reason.

Deferrals may be proposed by agencies but must be communicated to Congress by the President in a special message. Deferred budget authority may be withheld without further action by Congress. Congress may disapprove a deferral by law. A deferral may not extend beyond the end of the fiscal year of the budget authority's availability. However, for multiyear funds, the President may re-report the deferral the next fiscal year. Deferred budget authority that is disapproved by Congress must be made available immediately. Agencies must release all other deferred budget authority with sufficient time remaining in the fiscal year to prudently obligate that budget authority before the end of the fiscal year. (*See also* Apportionment; Budgetary Reserves; Impoundment; Rescission.)

DEFICIENCY APPORTIONMENT

As provided for in the Antideficiency Act (31 U.S.C. § 1515) an apportionment by the Office of Management and Budget (OMB) indicating the need for supplemental budget authority to permit payment of pay increases to civilian and military employees and military retirees as required by law. In addition, the head of an executive branch agency may request a deficiency apportionment if (1) a new law is enacted requiring unanticipated expenditures beyond administrative control or (2) an emergency arises involving the safety of human life or the protection of property. Approval for requests for such an apportionment does not authorize agencies to exceed available resources within an account. (*See also* Antideficiency Act; Apportionment; Deficiency Appropriation; Supplemental Appropriation.)

DEFICIENCY APPROPRIATION

An appropriation made to pay obligations for which sufficient funds are not available. The need often results from violations of the Antideficiency Act. Though technically distinct from a supplemental appropriation,

Congress has stopped passing separate deficiency appropriations and the distinction therefore has become obscured since the 1960s.

DEFICIT

The amount by which the government's spending exceeds its revenues for a given period, usually a fiscal year (opposite of surplus).

Budget Deficit

The amount by which the government's budget outlays exceed its budget receipts for a given period, usually a fiscal year. (*See also* Budget Surplus *under* Surplus.)

Unified Deficit/Total Deficit

The amount by which the government's on-budget and off-budget outlays exceed the sum of its on-budget and off-budget receipts for a given period, usually a fiscal year. (*See also* Budget Surplus *under* Surplus; Off-Budget.)

DEFLATION (ECONOMICS TERM)

A sustained decrease in the general price level.

DEFLATOR (ECONOMICS TERM)

An index used to adjust a current dollar amount to its real dollar counterpart, that is, to remove the effects of inflation. (*See also* Inflator.)

DEOBLIGATION

An agency's cancellation or downward adjustment of previously incurred obligations. Deobligated funds may be reobligated within the period of availability of the appropriation. For example, annual appropriated funds may be reobligated in the fiscal year in which the funds were appropriated, while multiyear or no-year appropriated funds may be reobligated in the same or subsequent fiscal years. (*See* Reobligation.)

DEPRECIATION

The systematic and rational allocation of the acquisition cost of an asset, less its estimated salvage or residual value, over its estimated useful life. Depreciation reflects the use of the asset(s) during specific operating periods in order to match costs with related revenues in measuring income or determining the costs of carrying out program activities.

DIRECT SPENDING

As defined by the Balanced Budget and Emergency Deficit Control Act of 1985, entitlement authority, the Food Stamp Program, and budget authority provided by law other than appropriations acts. Direct spending may be temporary or permanent, definite or indefinite (as to amount) but it is an appropriation or other budget authority made available to agencies in an act other than an appropriation act. Under expired Budget Enforcement Act (BEA) provisions, new direct spending was subject to pay-as-you-go (PAYGO) requirements. (*See also* Balanced Budget and Emergency Deficit Control Act of 1985; Entitlement Authority; Mandatory; Pay-as-You-Go. For a distinction, *see* Discretionary.)

DISBURSEMENTS

Amounts paid by federal agencies, by cash or cash equivalent, during the fiscal year to liquidate government obligations. "Disbursement" is used interchangeably with the term "outlay." In budgetary usage, gross disbursements represent the amount of checks issued and cash or other payments made, less refunds received. Net disbursements represent gross disbursements less income collected and credited to the appropriation or fund account, such as amounts received for goods and services provided. (*See also* Outlay; Expenditure.)

DISCOUNT RATE (ECONOMICS TERM)

One of the following:

(1) The interest rate used to determine the present value of a future stream of receipts and outlays, or in cost-benefit analysis, of benefits and costs. This use of the term is completely distinct from that in monetary policy, and the interest rates involved are generally not those charged by Federal Reserve Banks.

Discount rate policies of the three major oversight and budget agencies—the Government Accountability Office (GAO), the Office of Management and Budget (OMB), and the Congressional Budget Office (CBO)—are consistent with basic economic principles but vary significantly in their formulations for different analyses. GAO's *Discount Rate Policy* (GAO/OCE-17.1.1), May 1991, describes different approaches and their applications.

In estimating net present values under credit reform, discount rate represents the average interest rate on marketable Treasury securities of similar maturity to the cash flows of the direct loan or loan guarantee for which the estimate is being made. (*See* Credit Subsidy Cost *under* Federal Credit.)

(2) The interest rate that a commercial bank pays when it borrows from a Federal Reserve Bank. The discount rate is one of the tools of monetary policy used by the Federal Reserve System. The Federal Reserve customarily raises or lowers the discount rate to signal a shift toward restraining or easing its monetary and credit policy. (*See also* Monetary Policy.)

DISCRETIONARY

A term that usually modifies either "spending," "appropriation," or "amount." "Discretionary spending" refers to outlays from budget authority that is provided in and controlled by appropriation acts. "Discretionary appropriation" refers to those budgetary resources that are provided in appropriation acts, other than those that fund mandatory programs. "Discretionary amount" refers to the level of budget authority, outlays, or other budgetary resources (other than those which fund mandatory programs) that are provided in, and controlled by, appropriation acts. (*See also* Appropriation Act; Appropriations *under* Forms of Budget Authority *under* Budget Authority; One-Year Authority *under* Duration *under* Budget Authority; Gramm-Rudman-Hollings. For a contrast, *see* Entitlement Authority; Mandatory.)

E

EARMARKING

Either of the following:

(1) Dedicating collections by law for a specific purpose or program. Earmarked collections include trust fund receipts, special fund receipts, intragovernmental receipts, and offsetting collections credited to appropriation accounts. These collections may be classified as budget receipts, proprietary receipts, or reimbursements to appropriations.

(2) Designating any portion of a lump-sum amount for particular purposes by means of legislative language. Sometimes, "earmarking" is colloquially used to characterize directions included in congressional committee reports but not in the legislation itself. (*See also* Special Fund Accounts *under* Federal Fund Accounts *under* Account in the President's Budget; Trust Fund Accounts *under* Account in the President's

Budget; Offsetting Collections *under* Collections; Proprietary Receipts from the Public *under* Offsetting Receipts *under* Collections; Committee Allocation.)

ECONOMY ACT

A common reference to section 1535 of title 31 of the *United States Code* that provides general authority for one agency or unit thereof to obtain goods and services from another agency or unit. Payment may be made in advance or upon the provision of the goods and services ordered.

EMERGENCY

A term that usually modifies "appropriation," "legislation," or "supplemental." Under procedures typically prescribed in concurrent resolutions on the budget, the House or the Senate, or their respective committees of jurisdiction, may designate proposed appropriations or other legislation as "emergency legislation" and thereby exempt any new budget authority, outlays, or receipts resulting from such legislation from specified enforcement provisions in the Congressional Budget Act, the concurrent resolution itself, or both. (*See also* Appropriations *under* Forms of Budget Authority *under* Budget Authority.)

Acts appropriating funds for national or international emergencies such as natural disasters or urgent national security events are typically designated "emergency supplemental." (*See also* Supplemental Appropriation.)

ENTITLEMENT AUTHORITY

Authority to make payments (including loans and grants) for which budget authority is not provided in advance by appropriation acts to any person or government if, under the provisions of the law containing such authority, the U.S. government is legally required to make the payments to persons or governments that meet the requirements established by law (2 U.S.C. § 622(9)).

Under the Budget Enforcement Act (BEA), new entitlement authority was defined as direct spending and was subject to the pay-as-you-go (PAYGO) provisions. (*See also* Appropriated Entitlement; Authorizing Legislation; Backdoor Authority/Backdoor Spending; Budget Enforcement Act; Mandatory; Pay-as-You-Go.)

EXPENDITURE

The actual spending of money; an outlay.

EXPENSE

Outflow or other depletion of assets or incurrences of liabilities (or a combination of both) during some period as a result of providing goods, rendering services, or carrying out other activities related to an entity's programs and missions, the benefits from which do not extend beyond the present operating period.

EXPIRED ACCOUNT

An account within the Department of the Treasury to hold expired budget authority. The expired budget authority retains its fiscal year (or multiyear) identity for an additional 5 fiscal years. After the 5-year period has elapsed, all obligated and unobligated balances are canceled, the expired account is closed, and all remaining funds are returned to the general fund of the Treasury and are thereafter no longer available for any purpose. (*See* Expired Budget Authority *under* Availability for New Obligations *under* Budget Authority.)

F

FACTS II

The Federal Agencies' Centralized Trial-Balance System, managed by the Department of the Treasury's Financial Management Service (FMS) for the Office of Management and Budget (OMB). The system gathers quarterly budget execution information electronically, which is used to prepare Reports on Budget Execution (SF-133), Yearend Closing Statements (FMS-2108), and portions of the actual column of the President's budget.

FEDERAL ACCOUNTING STANDARDS ADVISORY BOARD (FASAB)

Sponsored under an agreement between the Department of the Treasury, the Office of Management and Budget (OMB), and Government

Accountability Office (GAO). FASAB promulgates Statements of Federal Financial Accounting Standards (SFFAS) after considering the financial and budgetary information needs of citizens, congressional oversight groups, executive agencies, and other users of federal financial information. See www.FASAB.gov. (For a discussion of the methods for tracking funds in the federal government, *see* app. III.)

FEDERAL CREDIT

Defined by the Federal Credit Reform Act of 1990 (FCRA) as federal direct loans and federal loan guarantees.

Administrative Expense

The cost that is directly related to credit program operations, including payments to contractors. The Federal Credit Reform Act of 1990 (FCRA) requires that administrative expenses for both direct loans and loan guarantees be included in program accounts. Administrative expenses are not included in subsidy costs appropriations but are separately appropriated.

Cohort

All direct loans or loan guarantees of a program for which a subsidy appropriation is provided for a given fiscal year, even when disbursements occur in subsequent fiscal years. For direct loans and loan guarantees that receive multiyear or no-year appropriations, the cohort is defined by the year of obligation. Pre-1992 direct loans that are modified will constitute a single cohort. Likewise, pre-1992 loan guarantees that are modified constitute a cohort. (*See also* Direct Loan *and* Guaranteed Loan *under* Federal Credit.)

Credit Reestimates

Recalculation of the estimated cost to the government of a group of direct loans or loan guarantees. After new direct loans or loan guarantees are made, the Federal Credit Reform Act of 1990 (FCRA) requires periodic revisions of the subsidy cost estimate of a cohort (or risk category) based on information about the actual performance, estimated changes in future cash flows of the cohort, or both. Reestimates must generally be made annually (with an associated recalculation of applicable cumulative interest), as long as any loans in the cohort are outstanding. These reestimates represent additional costs or savings to the government and are recorded in the budget. An upward reestimate indicates that insufficient funds had been paid to the financing account, so the increase (plus interest on reestimates) is paid from the program account to the financing account to make it whole. Permanent indefinite budget authority is available for this purpose. A downward reestimate indicates that too much subsidy had been paid to the financing account. The excess identified in a downward reestimate (plus interest) may be credited directly to the program account as offsetting collections for programs classified as mandatory or to a downward reestimate receipt account for programs classified as discretionary.

Credit Reform

The method of controlling and accounting for credit programs in the federal budget after fiscal year 1991. The Federal Credit Reform Act of 1990 (FCRA) added title V to the Congressional Budget Act of 1974. It requires that the credit subsidy cost be financed from new budget authority and be recorded as budget outlays at the time the direct or guaranteed loans are disbursed. In turn, it authorizes the creation of nonbudgetary financing accounts to receive this subsidy cost payment. Agencies must have appropriations for the subsidy cost before they can enter into direct loan obligations or loan guarantee commitments. (*See also* Credit Subsidy Cost, Direct Loan Obligation, Discount Rate, *and* Loan Guarantee Commitment *under* Federal Credit; Present Value.)

Risk Category

Subdivisions of a cohort of direct loans or loan guarantees that are relatively homogeneous in cost, given the facts known at the time of obligation or commitment. Risk categories will group within a cohort all direct loans or loan guarantees that share characteristics that predict defaults and other costs. They may be defined by characteristics or combinations of characteristics of the loan, the project financed, the borrower, or a combination of these.

Statistical evidence must be presented, based on historical analysis of program data or comparable credit data, concerning the likely costs of defaults, other deviations from contract, or other costs that are expected to be associated with the loans in that category.

Credit Reform Act Accounts

Credit Program Account
A budget account that receives and obligates appropriations to cover the subsidy cost (on a net present value basis) of a direct loan or loan guarantee and disburses the subsidy cost to the financing account. Usually, a separate amount is also appropriated in the program account for administrative expenses that are directly related to credit program operations. (*See also* Present Value.)

Financing Account
A nonbudgetary account (or accounts) associated with each credit program account that holds balances, receives the subsidy cost payment from the credit program account, and includes all other cash flows to and from the government resulting from direct loan obligations or loan guarantee commitments made on or after October 1, 1991. It disburses loans, collects repayments and fees, makes claim payments, holds balances, borrows from the Department of the Treasury, earns or pays interest, and receives the subsidy cost payment from the credit program account.

Liquidating Account
A budget account that includes all cash flows to and from the government resulting from direct loan obligations or loan guarantee commitments made prior to October 1, 1991. The Federal Credit Reform Act of 1990 (FCRA) requires that such accounts be shown in the budget on a cash basis. Agencies are required to transfer end-of-year unobligated balances in these accounts to the general fund as soon as practicable after the close of the fiscal year.

Negative Subsidy Receipt Account
A budget account for the receipt of amounts paid from the financing account when there is a negative subsidy for the original estimate. In most cases, the receipt account is a general fund receipt account and amounts are not earmarked for the credit program. They are available for appropriation

only in the sense that all general fund receipts are available for appropriation. Separate downward reestimate receipt accounts are used to record amounts paid from the financing account for downward reestimates.

Credit Subsidy Cost

The estimated long-term cost to the government of a direct loan or loan guarantee, calculated on a net present value basis and excluding administrative costs.

In estimating the net present value, for loans made, guaranteed, or modified in fiscal year 2001 and after, the cash flow estimated for each year (or other time period) is discounted using the interest rate on a marketable zero-coupon Treasury security with the same maturity from the date of disbursement as that cash flow. For loans made or guaranteed prior to fiscal year 2001, the discount rate is the average interest rate on marketable Treasury securities of similar maturity to the direct loan or loan guarantee for which the estimate is being made. The rate at which interest will be paid on the amounts borrowed or held as an uninvested balance by a financing account for a particular cohort is the same as the financial discount rate for a cohort, the disbursement-weighted average discount rate (for cohorts before 2001) or a single effective rate (for cohorts 2001 and after) derived from this collection of interest rates. (*See also* Credit Reform, Direct Loan, *and* Guaranteed Loan *under* Federal Credit; Present Value; Subsidy.)

Direct Loan Subsidy Cost

The estimated long-term cost to the government of a direct loan, excluding administrative costs. Specifically, the subsidy cost of a direct loan is the net present value, at the time when the direct loan is disbursed from the financing account, of the estimated loan disbursements, repayments of principal, payments of interest, recoveries or proceeds of asset sales, and other payments by or to the government over the life of the loan. These estimated cash flows include the effects of estimated defaults, prepayments, fees, penalties, and expected actions by the government and the borrower within the terms of the loan contract.

Guaranteed Loan Subsidy Cost

The estimated long-term cost to the government of a loan guarantee, excluding administrative costs. The Federal Credit Reform Act of 1990 (FCRA) specifies that the credit subsidy cost of a loan guarantee is the net present value, at the time a guaranteed loan is disbursed by the lender, of the following cash flows: (1) estimated payments by the government to cover defaults, delinquencies, interest subsidies, or other payments and (2) the estimated payments to the government, including origination and other fees, penalties, and recoveries.

Direct Loan

A disbursement of funds by the government to a nonfederal borrower under a contract that requires the repayment of such funds either with or without interest. The term includes the purchase of or the participation in a loan made by a lender; financing arrangements that defer payment for more than 90 days, including the sale of a government asset on credit terms; and loans financed by the Federal Financing Bank (FFB) pursuant to agency loan guarantee authority. It does not include the acquisition of federally guaranteed loans in satisfaction of default or other price support loans of the Commodity Credit Corporation. Under credit reform, the budget records the credit subsidy cost of direct loans as outlays. The subsidies are paid to the direct loan financing accounts, which, in turn, make the loans to the public. For more information, see Credit and Insurance and accompanying tables in the President's budget. (*See also* Asset Sale; Credit Reform, Credit Subsidy Cost, Direct Loan Obligation, *and* Guaranteed Loan *under* Federal Credit.)

Direct Loan Obligation

A binding agreement by a federal agency to make a direct loan when the borrower fulfills specified conditions.

Under credit reform, direct loan obligations are composed of obligations for both the credit subsidy cost and the unsubsidized amounts of the loan. When an agency enters into a direct loan obligation, it obligates itself to pay the credit subsidy cost to the direct loan financing account, and the financing account is committed to make the loan to the borrower. Only the credit subsidy cost is recorded as a budgetary obligation. (*See also* Direct Loan *under* Federal Credit.)

Guaranteed Loan

A nonfederal loan to which a federal guarantee is attached. The loan principal is recorded as a guaranteed loan regardless of whether the federal guarantee is full or partial. For the purposes of the Federal Credit Reform Act of 1990 (FCRA), a loan guarantee is defined as any guarantee, insurance, or other pledge with respect to the payment of all or a part of the principal or interest on any debt obligation of a nonfederal borrower to a nonfederal lender, but does not include the insurance of deposits, shares, or other withdrawable accounts in financial institutions. Under credit reform, the budget records the credit subsidy cost of guaranteed loans as outlays. The subsidies are paid to the guaranteed loan financing accounts, which hold these uninvested funds to serve as a reserve against future loan defaults or other payments to lenders. (*See also* Credit Reform, Direct Loan, *and* Loan Guarantee Commitment *under* Federal Credit.)

Loan Guarantee Commitment

A binding agreement by a federal agency to make a loan guarantee when specified conditions are fulfilled by the borrower, the lender, or any other party to the guarantee agreement. (*See also* Commitment; Credit Reform *and* Guaranteed Loan *under* Federal Credit.)

FEDERAL CREDIT REFORM ACT (FCRA)

See under Federal Credit.

Federal Financing Bank (FFB)

A government corporation created by the Federal Financing Bank Act of 1973 under the general supervision of the Secretary of the Treasury. FFB was established to (1) finance federal and federally assisted borrowings in ways that least disrupt private markets, (2) coordinate such borrowing programs with the government's overall fiscal policy, and (3) reduce the costs of such borrowing from the public.

FFB provides financial assistance to or on behalf of federal agencies by (1) making direct loans to federal agencies to help them fund their programs, (2) purchasing loan assets from federal agencies, and (3) making direct loans to nonfederal borrowers (including foreign governments) that are secured by federal agency guarantees against risk of default by borrowers on loan principal and interest payments. FFB obtains funds by borrowing from the Department of the Treasury. For more information, see www.treas.gov/ffb/.

FEEDER ACCOUNT

Appropriation and revolving fund accounts whose resources are available only for transfer to other specified appropriation or revolving fund accounts.

FINANCIAL ACCOUNTING

See under Proprietary Accounting.

FINANCIAL STATEMENTS

A document that describes an entity's financial activity and status for a specified period. Under federal law and applicable accounting standards, the financial statements for a federal agency usually include a balance sheet, statement of net cost, statement of changes in net position, statement of budgetary resources, and statement of financing.

FISCAL POLICY (ECONOMICS TERM)

Federal government policies with respect to taxes and spending that affect the level, composition, and distribution of national income and output. The budget process is a major vehicle for determining and implementing federal fiscal policy. Many summary indicators of fiscal policy exist. Some, such as the budget surplus or deficit, are narrowly budgetary. Others attempt to reflect aspects of how fiscal policy affects the economy.

FISCAL YEAR

Any yearly accounting period, regardless of its relationship to a calendar year. The fiscal year for the federal government begins on October 1 of each year and ends on September 30 of the following year; it is designated by the calendar year in which it ends. For example, fiscal year 1990 began October 1, 1989, and ended September 30, 1990. (Prior to fiscal year 1977, the federal fiscal year began on July 1 and ended on June 30. The 3-month period, July 1, 1976, to September 30, 1976, between fiscal years 1976 and 1977 is called the transition quarter ("TQ").) (For a more detailed description of the budget process, *see* app. I.)

Budget Year

A term used in the budget formulation process to refer to the fiscal year for which the budget is being considered, that is, with respect to a session of Congress, the fiscal year of the government that starts on October 1 of the calendar year in which that session of Congress begins.

Current Year

A term used in the budget formulation process to refer to the fiscal year immediately preceding the budget year under consideration.

Outyear

In the Concurrent Resolution on the Budget, or in the President's budget submission, any fiscal year (or years) beyond the budget year for which projections are made.

Prior Year

The fiscal year immediately preceding the current year.

Program Year

Describes the authorized operating period of a particular program. The term is usually used to distinguish the program's operating period from the federal government's fiscal year. For example, a program year may begin on July 1 of a year and end on June 30 of the following year. Thus, program year 2003 began on July 1, 2003, and ended on June 30, 2004.

FIXED APPROPRIATION ACCOUNT

An account in which appropriations are available for obligation for a definite period. A fixed appropriation account can receive appropriations available for obligation for 1 year (an annual account) or for a specified number of years (a multiyear account). (For a distinction, *see* No-Year Authority *under* Duration *under* Budget Authority.)

FORWARD FUNDING

Budget authority that is made available for obligation beginning in the last quarter of the fiscal year for the financing of ongoing activities (usually grant programs) during the next fiscal year. This funding is used mostly for education programs, so that obligations for grants can be made prior to the beginning of the next school year. (For a distinction, *see* Advance Appropriation; Advance Funding; Multiple-Year Authority *under* Duration *under* Budget Authority.)

FRANCHISE FUND

A type of intragovernmental revolving fund that operates as a self-supporting entrepreneurial entity to provide common administrative services benefiting other federal entities. These funds function entirely from the fees charged for the services they provide consistent with their statutory authority. (*See also* Intragovermental Revolving Fund Account *under* Intragovernmental Fund Account *under* Federal Fund Accounts *under* Account in the President's Budget.)

FTE (FULL-TIME EQUIVALENT)

Reflects the total number of regular straight-time hours (i.e., not including overtime or holiday hours) worked by employees divided by the number of compensable hours applicable to each fiscal year. Annual leave, sick leave, and compensatory time off and other approved leave categories are considered to be "hours worked" for purposes of defining FTE employment.

FULL FUNDING

The provision of budgetary resources to cover the total estimated cost of a program or project at the time it is undertaken (regardless of when the funds will actually be obligated). Full funding generally pertains to the acquisition of capital assets, such as the construction of Navy ships or buildings to house federal agencies. (For a distinction, *see* Incremental Funding. *See also* Multiple-Year Authority *under* Duration *under* Budget Authority; Multiyear Budget Planning.)

The term full funding can sometimes refer to the appropriation of the total amount authorized by law. A program is said to be "fully funded" when the appropriation equals the authorized level or when appropriations are sufficient to cover service for all eligible persons or organizations.

FUNCTIONAL CLASSIFICATION

A system of classifying budget authority, outlays, receipts, and tax expenditures according to the national needs being addressed. Each concurrent resolution on the budget allocates budget authority and outlays among the various functions.

Each budget account appears in the single budget function (for example, national defense or health) that best reflects its major purpose, an important national need. A function may be divided into two or more subfunctions, depending upon the complexity of the national need addressed. (*See also* Budget Activity.)

FUND ACCOUNTING

Commonly used to refer to the administrative system of funds control that each agency establishes to ensure compliance with federal fiscal laws. The statutory basis for fund accounting is found primarily in the requirement of the Antideficiency Act that the head of each agency prescribe, by regulation, a system of funds control (31 U.S.C. § 1514(a)). (*See also* Antideficiency Act.)

G

GDP (GROSS DOMESTIC PRODUCT) (ECONOMICS TERM)

The value of all final goods and services produced within the borders of a country such as the United States in a given period, whether produced by residents or nonresidents. The components of GDP are personal consumption expenditures, gross private domestic investment, net exports of goods and services, and government consumption expenditures and gross investment. That value is conceptually equal to the sum of incomes generated within the borders of the country in the same time period. (*See also* GNP; National Income and Product Accounts.)

GDP PRICE INDEX (ECONOMICS TERM)

A measure of the price level for the whole economy covering the prices of goods and services produced in a country such as the United States.

GENERATIONAL ACCOUNTING

Estimates who pays for all that the government buys. Generational accounts estimate the real (inflation-adjusted) net taxes to be paid by the average member of each generation (today's newborns, 1-year-olds, and so on). They also estimate the net taxes of the average member of the representative future generation (those not yet born). The accounts project government purchases and net taxes of current generations and calculate their present values.

Generational accounts do not try to estimate who benefits from what the government buys, only who pays for it with their net taxes. They do not try to predict the actual course of policy. Generational accounts act as a gauge, not a predictor or goal. They do not try to say how policy will actually evolve. And they cannot say what distributions are fair; that is a matter of policy, not analysis. The accounts serve only as a norm by which to evaluate prevailing policy and compare alternative policies.

GNP (GROSS NATIONAL PRODUCT) (ECONOMICS TERM)

The value of all final goods and services produced by labor and capital supplied by residents of a country such as the United States in a given period, whether or not the residents are located within the country. That value is conceptually equal to the sum of incomes accruing to residents of the country in the same time period. GNP differs from GDP in that GNP includes net receipts of income from the rest of the world while GDP excludes them. (*See also* GDP; National Income and Product Accounts.)

GOVERNMENT PERFORMANCE AND RESULTS ACT (GPRA)

The Government Performance and Results Act of 1993. GPRA, also known as the Results Act, intends to improve the efficiency and effectiveness of federal programs by requiring federal agencies to develop strategic plans, annual performance plans, and annual program performance reports.

GOVERNMENT-SPONSORED ENTERPRISE (GSE)

A privately owned and operated federally chartered financial institution that facilitates the flow of investment funds to specific economic sectors. GSEs, acting as financial intermediaries, provide these sectors access to national capital markets. The activities of GSEs are not included in the federal budget's totals because they are classified as private entities. However, because of their relationship to the government, detailed statements of financial operations and conditions are presented as supplementary information in the budget document. For the purposes of the Congressional Budget Act of 1974, as amended (2 U.S.C. § 622(8)), an entity must meet certain criteria to qualify as a GSE. (For distinctions, *see* Mixed-Ownership Government Corporation; Off-Budget; Wholly-Owned Government Corporation.)

GPRA

See under Government Performance and Results Act.

GRAMM-RUDMAN-HOLLINGS (GRH)

The popular name of the Balanced Budget and Emergency Deficit Control Act of 1985, so named for the Senate sponsors: Senators Phil Gramm, Warren Rudman, and Ernest F. Hollings. The act, a mechanism for reducing the federal deficit, set declining deficit targets for the federal government and established an automatic enforcement mechanism called sequestration. GRH has been amended several times, most significantly by the Budget Enforcement Act of 1990 (BEA) and the Balanced Budget Act of 1997. (*See also* Budget Enforcement Act; Discretionary; Limitation; Mandatory; Sequestration.)

GRANT

A federal financial assistance award making payment in cash or in kind for a specified purpose. The federal government is not expected to have substantial involvement with the state or local government or other recipient while the contemplated activity is being performed. The term "grant" is used broadly and may include a grant to nongovernmental recipients as well as one to a state or local government, while the term "grant-in-aid" is commonly used to refer only to a grant to a state or local government. (For a more detailed description, *see* the Federal Grant and Cooperative Agreement

Act of 1977, 31 U.S.C. §§ 6301–6308.) The two major forms of federal grants-in-aid are block and categorical.

Block grants are given primarily to general purpose governmental units in accordance with a statutory formula. Such grants can be used for a variety of activities within a broad functional area. Examples of federal block grant programs are the Omnibus Crime Control and Safe Streets Act of 1968, the Housing and Community Development Act of 1974, and the grants to states for social services under title XX of the Social Security Act.

Categorical grants can be used only for specific programs or for narrowly defined activities. They may be formula or project grants. Formula grants allocate federal funds to states or their subdivisions in accordance with a distribution formula prescribed by law or administrative regulation. Project grants provide federal funding for fixed or known periods for specific projects or the delivery of specific services or products.

I

IDENTIFICATION CODE

Each appropriation or fund account in the President's budget carries an 11-digit code that identifies (1) the agency, (2) the account, (3) the nature or timing of the transmittal to Congress (for example, regular budget cycle or supplemental), (4) the type of fund, and (5) the account's functional and subfunctional classifications. (For a detailed explanation of the account identification code, *see* app. V.)

IMPLICIT PRICE DEFLATOR (ECONOMICS TERM)

Weighted averages of the most detailed price indexes used in estimating real output. Before 1995, implicit price deflators were calculated as the ratio of current- to constant-dollar output multiplied by 100. Since 1995, implicit price deflators have been calculated as the ratio of current- to chained-dollar output multiplied by 100. For all but the most recent estimates, the implicit price deflators are identical to the chain-type price indexes because the weights used to aggregate the detailed prices for the two measures are the same. Implicit price deflators are used in the National Income and Product Accounts (NIPA). (*See also* Chain Price Indexes; Chained Dollars.)

IMPOUNDMENT

Any action or inaction by an officer or employee of the federal government that precludes obligation or expenditure of budget authority. There are two types of impoundments: deferrals and proposed rescissions. Not all delays in obligating funds are deferrals. Sometimes obligation delays are due to legitimate programmatic reasons or the result of outside forces not under the agency's control; for example, an agency administering a grant program receives no grant applications so no grants can be made. (*See also* Congressional Budget and Impoundment Control Act of 1974; Deferral of Budget Authority; Rescission.)

INCREMENTAL FUNDING

The provision or recording of budgetary resources for a program or project based on obligations estimated to be incurred within a fiscal year when such budgetary resources are provided for only part of the estimated cost of the acquisition. (For a distinction, *see* Full Funding.)

INFLATION (ECONOMICS TERM)

A rise in the general price level.

INFLATOR (ECONOMICS TERM)

An index used to express a current dollar amount in prices of another period.

INTERNAL CONTROL

An integral component of an organization's management that provides reasonable assurance that the following objectives are being achieved: (1) effectiveness and efficiency of operations, (2) reliability of financial reporting, and (3) compliance with applicable laws and regulations. Safeguarding of assets is a subset of all three of these objectives.

J

JOINT RESOLUTION

A form of legislation (designated with S.J. Res. or H.J. Res.) that is either:

(1) A congressional action typically used in dealing with matters such as a single appropriation for a specific purpose, increasing the statutory limit on the public debt, or continuing appropriations. There is no real difference between a bill and a joint resolution; both require a majority vote and become law in the same manner, that is, by bicameral enactment and signature of the President.

(2) A congressional action used to propose amendments to the Constitution. Adoption of a joint resolution to propose a constitutional amendment requires a two-thirds majority vote by both the Senate and the House and is not presented to the President for approval. A proposed amendment becomes effective only when ratified by three-fourths of the states.

(*See also* Continuing Appropriation/Continuing Resolution. For a distinction, *see* Concurrent Resolution on the Budget.)

JUSTIFICATION

The documents an agency submits to the appropriations committees in support of its budget request. The Office of Management and Budget (OMB) prescribes justification materials, which typically explain changes between the current appropriation and the amounts requested for the next fiscal year.

L

LEASE-PURCHASE

An agreement between a lessor and lessee in which the lessee agrees to lease a building or other property for a specified length of time and then takes title to the building or other property at the end of the lease period. (*See also* Capital Lease; Operating Lease.)

LIABILITY

Defined differently for obligational (or budgetary) and proprietary (or financial) accounting purposes (*see* app. III).

Obligational (or budgetary) accounting, designed to ensure compliance with fiscal laws, is based on the concept of *legal* liability. A legal liability is a claim that may be legally enforced against the government. It may be created in a variety of ways, such as by signing a contract, grant, or cooperative agreement or by operation of law. (*See also* Obligation.)

Proprietary (or financial) accounting, designed to generate data for financial statement purposes, is based on the concept of *accounting* liability. For federal financial accounting purposes, a liability is a probable future outflow or other sacrifice of resources as a result of past transactions or events. Generally, liabilities are thought of as amounts owed for items or services received, assets acquired, construction performed (regardless of whether invoices have been received), an amount received but not yet earned, or other expenses incurred. (*See also* Contingent Liability.)

LIFE-CYCLE COSTS

The overall estimated cost, both government and contractor, for a particular program alternative over the time period corresponding to the life of the program, including direct and indirect initial costs plus any periodic or continuing costs of operation and maintenance.

LIMITATION

A restriction on the amount, purpose, or period of availability of budget authority. While limitations are most often established through appropriations acts, they may also be established through authorization legislation. Limitations may be placed on the availability of funds for program levels, administrative expenses, direct loan obligations, loan guarantee commitments, or other purposes. (*See also* Administrative Division or Subdivision of Funds; Apportionment; Appropriation Act; Appropriation Rider; Authorizing Legislation; Duration *under* Budget Authority.)

LINE ITEM

In executive budgeting, a particular expenditure, such as program, subprogram, or object class. For purposes of the concurrent budget resolution, it usually refers to assumptions about particular programs or accounts implicit but not explicit in the budget resolution. In appropriation acts, it usually refers to an individual account or part of an account for which a specific amount is available. (*See also* Line Item Veto; Obligated Balance *under* Obligational Authority; Appropriation Rider.)

LINE ITEM VETO

A phrase used to describe an executive power to veto or "cross out" only certain parts of legislation while allowing the rest of the legislation to become law. At the federal level, legislation granting the President a line item veto has been declared unconstitutional. The line item veto exists at the state level because their constitutions grant the power to the governors in forms that vary from state to state. Some states only permit line item vetoes in bills appropriating money.

Several legislative initiatives have been introduced in Congress over the years to give the President expanded or enhanced rescission or line item veto authority. In 1996 the Line Item Veto Act was enacted authorizing the President, after signing a bill into law, to cancel in whole any dollar amount of discretionary budget authority, any item of new direct spending, or any limited tax benefit if the President made certain determinations. In 1998, the United States Supreme Court in *Clinton v. City of New York*, 524 U.S. 417 (1998), held that the Line Item Veto Act violated the Presentment Clause, article 1, section 7, of the U.S. Constitution. Under that clause, the President must accept or veto in its entirety any bill passed by Congress. Granting the President line item veto authority would require a constitutional amendment. See also "Account" in the Department of the Treasury's Annual Report Appendix. (*See also* Discretionary; Enhanced Rescission *and* Expedited Rescission *under* Rescission; Line Item; Mandatory; Separate Enrollment.)

LIQUIDATING APPROPRIATION

An appropriation to pay obligations incurred pursuant to substantive legislation, usually contract authority. A liquidating appropriation is not recorded as budget authority.

LOCKBOX

In the budget context, any of several legislative mechanisms that attempt to isolate, or "lock away," funds of the federal government for purposes such as reducing federal spending, preserving surpluses, or protecting the solvency of trust funds.

M

MANDATORY

A term that usually modifies either "spending" or "amount." "Mandatory spending," also known as "direct spending," refers to budget authority that is provided in laws other than appropriation acts and the outlays that result from such budget authority. Mandatory spending includes entitlement authority (for example, the Food Stamp, Medicare, and veterans' pension programs), payment of interest on the public debt, and nonentitlements such as payments to states from Forest Service receipts. By defining eligibility and setting the benefit or payment rules, Congress controls spending for these programs indirectly rather than directly through appropriations acts. "Mandatory amount" refers to the level of budget authority, outlays, or other budgetary resources that are controlled by laws other than appropriations acts. Budget authority provided in annual appropriations acts for certain programs is treated as mandatory because the authorizing legislation entitles beneficiaries to receive payment or otherwise obligates the government to make payment. (*See also* Appropriated Entitlement; Appropriations *under* Forms of Budget Authority *under* Budget Authority; Multiple-Year Authority *and* No-Year Authority *under* Duration *under* Budget Authority; Committee Allocation; Direct Spending Authority; Discretionary; Entitlement Authority; Gramm-Rudman-Hollings.)

MARK-UP

Meetings where congressional committees work on language of bills or resolutions. For example, at Budget Committee mark-ups, the House and Senate Budget Committees work on the language and numbers contained in budget resolutions and legislation affecting the congressional budget process.

MEANS OF FINANCING

Ways in which a budget deficit is financed or a budget surplus is used. A budget deficit may be financed by the Department of the Treasury (Treasury) (or agency) borrowing, by reducing Treasury cash balances, by the sale of gold, by seigniorage, by net cash flows resulting from transactions in credit financing accounts, by allowing certain unpaid liabilities to increase, or by other similar transactions. It is customary to separate total means of financing into "change in debt held by the public" (the government's debt, which is the primary means of financing) and "other means of financing" (seigniorage, change in cash balances, transactions of credit financing accounts, etc.). (*See also* Debt, Federal; Debt Service; Financing Account *under* Credit Reform Accounts *under* Federal Credit; Seigniorage.)

MID-SESSION REVIEW OF THE BUDGET

A supplemental summary and update of the budget that the President submitted to Congress in January or February of that year. Section 1106 of title 31 of the *United States Code* requires the mid-session review to contain revised estimates of budget receipts, outlays, and budget authority and other summary information and that it be issued by July 15 of each year. (*See also* Budget Update.)

MIXED-OWNERSHIP GOVERNMENT CORPORATION

An enterprise or business activity designated by the Government Corporation Control Act (31 U.S.C. § 9101) or some other statute as a mixed-ownership government corporation. The fiscal activities of some mixed-ownership government corporations appear in the budget. The Federal Deposit Insurance Corporation (FDIC) is an example of such a corporation. (For distinctions, *see* Government-Sponsored Enterprise; Off-Budget; Wholly-Owned Government Corporation.)

MONETARY POLICY (ECONOMICS TERM)

A policy affecting the money supply, interest rates, and credit availability that is intended to achieve maximum sustainable output and employment and to promote stable prices (interpreted as a low-inflation environment in practice). Monetary policy is directed by the Federal Reserve System. It functions by influencing the cost and availability of bank reserves through (1) open-market operations (the purchase and sale of securities, primarily Treasury securities), (2) changes in the ratio of reserves to deposits that commercial banks are required to maintain, (3) changes in the discount rate, and (4) changes in the federal fund rate. (*See also* Discount Rate; Fiscal Policy.)

MONEY SUPPLY (ECONOMICS TERM)

Anything that is generally accepted in payment for goods and services or in the repayment of debt. Narrow definitions of the money supply include currency and checking accounts, while broader definitions include other types of assets, such as savings deposits and money market mutual funds.

MONTHLY TREASURY STATEMENT (MTS)

A summary statement prepared from agency accounting reports and issued by the Department of the Treasury (Treasury). The MTS presents the receipts, outlays, resulting budget surplus or deficit, and federal debt for the month and the fiscal year to date and a comparison of those figures to those of the same period in the previous year. Treasury also issues the Daily Treasury Statement (DTS), which is published every working day of the federal government. It provides data on Treasury's cash and debt operations.

MULTIYEAR BUDGET PLANNING

A process—such as the one used to develop the President's budget and the congressional budget resolution—designed to ensure that the longer range consequences of budget decisions are identified and reflected in the budget totals. The President's (or executive) budget includes multiyear planning estimates for budget authority, outlays, and receipts for 4 years beyond the budget year. As of the date of this glossary, the congressional budget resolution provided budget totals for the budget year and, at least, each of the 4 succeeding fiscal years. This process provides a structure for the review and analysis of long-term program and tax policy choices.

The Office of Management and Budget (OMB) planning estimates are either presidential policy or current services estimates. Presidential policy estimates represent projections or extrapolations of likely outcomes based upon current law and enunciated administration policy. In some cases, outyear presidential policy estimates represent outyear policy rather than an extrapolation from budget-year policy. Current services estimates represent projections of possible outcomes based on the continuation of existing levels of service without policy changes. (*See also* Current Services Estimates; Full Funding; Outyear *under* Fiscal Year; Projections.)

N

NATIONAL INCOME AND PRODUCT ACCOUNTS (NIPA) (ECONOMICS TERM)

The comprehensive set of accounts prepared and published by the Department of Commerce that measures the total value of goods and services (gross domestic product, or GDP) produced by the U.S. economy and the total income earned in producing that output.

NET PRESENT VALUE (ECONOMICS TERM)

The present value of the estimated future cash inflows minus the present value of the cash outflows.

NOMINAL DOLLAR (ECONOMICS TERM)

See under Current Dollar.

NONBUDGETARY

A term used to refer to transactions of the government that do not belong within the budget. Nonbudgetary transactions (such as deposit funds, direct loan and loan guarantee financing accounts, and seigniorage) do not belong in the budget because they do not represent net budget authority or outlays, but rather are means of financing. This contrasts with "off-budget," which refers to activities that are budgetary in nature but are required by law to be excluded from the budget. (*See* Off-Budget; Means of Financing.)

O

OBJECT CLASSIFICATION

A uniform classification identifying the obligations of the federal government by the types of goods or services purchased (such as personnel compensation, supplies and materials, and equipment) without regard to the agency involved or the purpose of the programs for which they are used. If the obligations are in a single object classification category, the classification is identified in the Program and Financing Schedule in the President's budget. For the activities distributed among two or more object classification categories, the budget has a separate object classification schedule to show the distribution of the obligations by object classification. See also Explanation of Estimates in the "Detailed Budget Estimates" section of the President's budget. General instructions are provided in OMB Circular No. A-11, revised. (*See also* Allocation. For a distinction, *see* Functional Classification.)

OBLIGATION

A definite commitment that creates a legal liability of the government for the payment of goods and services ordered or received, or a legal duty on the part of the United States that could mature into a legal liability by virtue of actions on the part of the other party beyond the control of the United States. Payment may be made immediately or in the future. An agency incurs an obligation, for example, when it places an order, signs a contract, awards a grant, purchases a service, or takes other actions that require the government to make payments to the public or from one government account to another. The standards for the proper reporting of obligations are found in section 1501(a) of title 31 of the *United States Code*. See also OMB Circular No. A-11.

OBLIGATION LIMITATION

See under Limitation.

OBLIGATIONAL ACCOUNTING

The accounting systems, processes, and people involved in collecting financial information necessary to control, monitor, and report on all funds made available to federal entities by legislation, including permanent, indefinite appropriations as well as appropriations enacted in annual and supplemental appropriations laws that may be available for one or multiple fiscal years. It is through obligational accounting that agencies ensure compliance with fiscal laws, including the Antideficiency Act and statutes related to the purpose and period of availability of appropriations.

Obligational accounting rests on the central concepts of the "obligation" and "disbursement" of public funds, as those terms are defined in this glossary. The Antideficiency Act, codified in part at sections 1341, 1514, and 1517, and the provisions of section 1501 (commonly referred to as the recording statute) of the *United States Code* provide the fundamental components of obligational accounting. Obligational accounting is sometimes also referred to as "fund control accounting," "appropriation accounting," and "budgetary accounting." (For a discussion of the method for tracking funds in the federal government, *see* app. III. *See also* Administrative Division or Subdivision of Funds; Antideficiency Act; Apportionment; Disbursements; Obligation.)

OBLIGATIONAL AUTHORITY

The sum of (1) budget authority enacted for a given fiscal year, (2) unobligated balances of amounts that have not expired brought forward from prior years, (3) amounts of offsetting collections to be credited and available to specific funds or accounts during that year, and (4) budget authority transferred from other funds or accounts. The balance of obligational authority is an amount carried over from one year to the next if the budget authority is available for obligation in the next fiscal year. Not all obligational authority that becomes available in a fiscal year is obligated and paid out in that same year. Balances are described as (1) obligated, (2) unobligated, or (3) unexpended.

Obligated Balance

The amount of obligations already incurred for which payment has not yet been made. Technically, the obligated balance is the unliquidated obligations. Budget authority that is available for a fixed period expires at the end of its period of availability, but the obligated balance of the budget authority remains available to liquidate obligations for 5 additional fiscal years. At the end of the fifth fiscal year, the account is closed and any remaining balance is canceled. Budget authority available for an indefinite period may be canceled, and its account closed if (1) it is specifically rescinded by law or (2) the head of the agency concerned or the President determines that the purposes for which the appropriation was made have been carried out and disbursements have not been made from the appropriation for 2 consecutive years. (*See also* Duration *under* Budget Authority; Fixed Appropriation Account.)

Unobligated Balance

The portion of obligational authority that has not yet been obligated. For an appropriation account that is available for a fixed period, the budget authority expires after the period of availability ends but its unobligated balance remains available for 5 additional fiscal years for recording and adjusting obligations properly chargeable to the appropriations period of availability. For example, an expired, unobligated balance remains available until the account is closed to record previously unrecorded obligations or to make upward adjustments in previously underrecorded obligations, such as contract modifications properly within scope of the original contract. At the end of the fifth fiscal year, the account is closed and any remaining balance is canceled. For a no-year account, the unobligated balance is carried forward indefinitely until (1) specifically rescinded by law or (2) the head of the agency concerned or the President determines that the purposes for which the appropriation was made have been carried out and disbursements have not been made from the appropriation for 2 consecutive years. (*See also* Duration *under* Budget Authority; Expired Account; Expired Budget Authority *under* Availability for New Obligations *under* Budget Authority; Fixed Appropriation Account.)

Unexpended Balance

The sum of the obligated and unobligated balances.

OFF-BUDGET

Those budgetary accounts (either federal or trust funds) designated by law as excluded from budget totals. As of the date of this glossary, the revenues and outlays of the two Social Security trust funds (the Old-Age and Survivors Insurance Trust Fund and the Disability Insurance Trust Fund) and the transactions of the Postal Service are the only off-budget accounts. The budget documents routinely report the on-budget and off-budget amounts separately and then add them together to arrive at the consolidated government totals. (*See also* Nonbudgetary; On-Budget; Outlay; Trust Fund Expenditure Account *under* Trust Fund Accounts *under* Account in the President's Budget; Unified Budget.)

OMB CIRCULAR NO. A-11

Document that provides detailed guidance to executive departments and establishments by the Office of Management and Budget (OMB) for preparing and submitting the President's budget and executing the budget.

ON-BUDGET

All budgetary accounts other than those designated by law as off-budget. (*See also* Off-Budget.)

OPERATING BUDGET

A detailed projection of all estimated income and expenses during a given future period.

OPERATING LEASE

An agreement conveying the right to use property for a limited time in exchange for periodic payments. Operating lease criteria are ownership of the asset remains with lessor, the lease does not contain a bargain-price purchase option, the lease term does not exceed 75 percent of the estimated economic life of the asset, the present value of the minimum lease payments over the life of the lease does not exceed 90 percent of the fair market value of the asset at the beginning of the lease term, the asset is a general purpose asset rather than being for a special purpose of the government and is not built to the unique specification of the government as lessee, and there is a private sector market for the asset. (*See also* Capital Lease.)

OUTLAY

The issuance of checks, disbursement of cash, or electronic transfer of funds made to liquidate a federal obligation. Outlays also occur when interest on the Treasury debt held by the public accrues and when the government issues bonds, notes, debentures, monetary credits, or other cash-equivalent instruments in order to liquidate obligations. Also, under credit reform, the credit subsidy cost is recorded as an outlay when a direct or guaranteed loan is disbursed. An outlay is not recorded for repayment of debt principal, disbursements to the public by federal credit programs for direct loan obligations and loan guarantee commitments made in fiscal year 1992 or later, disbursements from deposit funds, and refunds of receipts that result from overpayments.

Outlays during a fiscal year may be for payment of obligations incurred in prior years (prior-year obligations) or in the same year. Outlays, therefore, flow in part from unexpended balances of prior-year budgetary resources and in part from budgetary resources provided for the year in which the money is spent.

Outlays are stated both gross and net of offsetting collections. (*See* Offsetting Collections *under* Collections.) Total government outlays include outlays of off-budget federal entities. (*See also* Expenditure; Expense.)

OUTYEAR

See under Fiscal Year.

OVERSIGHT COMMITTEE

The congressional committee charged with general oversight of an agency's or program's operations. In most cases, the oversight committee for an agency or program is also its authorizing committee. The Senate Committee on Homeland Security and Governmental Affairs and the House Committee on Government Reform also have general oversight on budget and accounting measures other than appropriations, except as provided in the Congressional Budget Act of 1974. (*See also* Authorizing Committee.)

P

PAY-AS-YOU-GO (PAYGO)

A budgetary enforcement mechanism originally set forth in the Budget Enforcement Act (BEA), which effectively expired at the end of fiscal year 2002. Under this mechanism, proposed changes in, or new permanent, law were expected to be deficit neutral in the aggregate in the fiscal year of enactment or in a period of years. PAYGO was intended to control growth in direct spending and tax legislation. The Senate, in the concurrent resolution on the budget, has established an internal rule enforcing a requirement that direct spending or receipts legislation under consideration in the Senate be deficit neutral over certain periods of time. This Senate PAYGO rule is enforced by points of order. (*See also* Point of Order; Sequestration.)

PERFORMANCE BUDGETING

Generally understood to refer to the infusion of performance information into the resource allocation process used to develop budget proposals or to execute an agreed-upon budget. Also known as results-based budgeting. (*See* Government Performance and Results Act.)

Agency Mission Statement

Defines the basic purpose, major functions, and operations of the agency. (*See* Strategic Plan *under* Performance Budgeting.)

Outcome Measure

An assessment of the result, effect, or consequence that will occur from carrying out a program or activity compared to its intended purpose.

Output Goal

A description of the level of activity or effort that will be produced or provided over a period or by a specified date, including a description of the characteristics and attributes (e.g., timeliness) established as standards in the course of conducting the activity or effort.

Output Measure

The level of activity or effort of a program (i.e., the products and services delivered) over a period that can be expressed quantitatively or qualitatively.

Performance and Accountability Report (PAR)

Provides financial and performance information that enables Congress, the President, and the public to assess the performance of an organization relative to its mission and for management to be accountable for its actions and resources. The Office of Management and Budget (OMB) provides guidance on the contents of the PARs, which integrate the reporting requirements of several laws, including (1) the Chief Financial Officers Act of 1990, (2) the Federal Managers' Financial Integrity Act of 1982, (3) the Government Management Reform Act of 1994, (4) the Government Performance and Results Act (GPRA) of 1993, and (5) the Reports Consolidation Act of 2000.

Performance Budget

A presentation that links strategic goals with related long-term and annual performance goals and with the costs of specific activities that contribute to the achievement of those goals.

Performance Goal

A target level of performance expressed as a tangible, measurable objective, against which actual achievement can be compared, including a goal expressed as a quantitative standard, value, or rate.

Performance Measure/Performance Indicator

A particular value or characteristic used to measure output, outcome, or efficiency of an organization or program. Performance measures are associated with performance goals in the annual performance plan.

Performance Plan

A plan that covers each program activity set forth in an agency's budget. It establishes performance goals to define the level of performance to be achieved by a program activity; expresses such goals in an objective, quantifiable, and measurable form; briefly describes the operational processes, skills, technology, and resources required to meet the performance goals; establishes performance indicators to be used in measuring or assessing the relevant outputs, service levels, and outcomes of each program activity; provides a basis for comparing actual program results with the established performance goals; and describes the means to be used to verify and validate measured values.

Performance Report

A report that sets forth the performance indicators established in the agency performance plan under the Government Performance and Results Act (GPRA) of 1993, along with the actual program performance achieved compared with the performance goals expressed in the plan for that fiscal year.

Program Activity

A specific activity or project as listed in the program and financing schedules of the President's budget.

Strategic Goal/Strategic Objective

A statement of aim or purpose included in a strategic plan (required under the Government Performance and Results Act (GPRA) of 1993) that defines how an agency will carry out a major segment of its mission over a certain period. The goal is expressed in a manner that allows a future assessment to be made of whether the goal was or is being achieved. In a performance budget/performance plan, strategic goals should be used to group multiple program outcome goals; the program outcome goals should relate to and in the aggregate be sufficient to influence the strategic goals or objectives and their performance measures.

Strategic Plan

Federal agency plan containing the organization's comprehensive mission statement, general goals and objectives, description of how the goals and objectives are to be achieved, description of how performance goals are related to the general goals and objectives, identification of key external factors, and description of program evaluations used to establish the general goals and objectives. Strategic plans must cover a period of not less than 5 years and must be updated and revised at least every 3 years.

PERFORMANCE MEASUREMENT

The ongoing monitoring and reporting of program accomplishments, particularly progress toward preestablished goals. It is typically conducted by program or agency management.

Performance measures may address the type or level of program activities conducted (process), the direct products and services delivered by a program (outputs), or the results of those products and services (outcomes).

A program may be any activity, project, function, or policy that has an identifiable purpose or set of objectives. (*See also* Performance Budgeting; Government Performance and Results Act.)

POINT OF ORDER

An objection raised on the House or Senate floor or in committees to an action being taken as contrary to that body's rules. In the House, for example, a point of order may be raised under Rule XXI objecting to an appropriation in an appropriation bill that was not previously authorized by law.

Many of the rules established in the Congressional Budget Act and related rules preclude the consideration of legislation that would violate totals in the budget resolutions, spending limits, or committee allocations. These rules are typically enforced through points of order. Points of order may be waived by a majority vote in the House. In the Senate, only points of order under the Budget Act may be waived (not points of order against actions that violate the Senate's standing rules), but the waiver generally requires a three-fifths vote. (*See also* Concurrent Resolution on the Budget; Congressional Budget Act.)

PRESENT VALUE (ECONOMICS TERM)

The worth of a future stream of returns or costs in terms of money paid immediately (or at some designated date). (Differs from Net Present Value.) A dollar available at some date in the future is worth less than a dollar available today because the latter could be invested at interest in the interim. In calculating present value, prevailing interest rates provide the basis for converting future amounts into their "money now" equivalents. (*See also* Discount Rate; Net Present Value.)

PRESIDENT'S BUDGET

The document sent to Congress by the President in January or February of each year, as required by law (31 U.S.C. § 1105), requesting new budget authority for federal programs and estimating federal revenues and outlays for the upcoming fiscal year and 4 subsequent outyears. Although the title of the document is *Budget of the U.S. Government*, it represents proposals for congressional consideration. (*See also* Budget; app. I.)

PROGRAM

Generally, an organized set of activities directed toward a common purpose or goal that an agency undertakes or proposes to carry out its responsibilities. Because the term has many uses in practice, it does not have a well-defined, standard meaning in the legislative process. It is used to describe an agency's mission, functions, activities, services, projects, and processes. (*See also* Program, Project, or Activity.)

PROGRAM ACCOUNT

See under Credit Program Account *under* Credit Reform Act Accounts *under* Federal Credit.

PROGRAM AND FINANCING SCHEDULE

A schedule published in the President's budget "Detailed Budget Estimates" presenting budget data by each appropriation or fund account. The schedule consists of eight sections: (1) obligations by program activity; (2) budgetary resources available for obligation; (3) new budget authority (gross), detail; (4) change in obligated balances; (5) outlays (gross), detail; (6) offsets to gross budget authority and outlays; (7) net budget authority and outlays; (8) and memorandum (non add) entries. (For a detailed discussion of the program and financing schedule, *see* app. VI. *See also* Account in the President's Budget.)

PROGRAM EVALUATION

An individual systematic study conducted periodically or on an ad hoc basis to assess how well a program is working. It is often conducted by experts external to the program, either inside or outside the agency, as well as by program managers. A program evaluation typically examines achievement of program objectives in the context of other aspects of program performance or in the context in which it occurs. (*See also* Performance Budgeting; Performance and Accountability Report *under* Performance Budgeting; Government Performance and Results Act.)

PROGRAM, PROJECT, OR ACTIVITY (PPA)

An element within a budget account. For annually appropriated accounts, the Office of Management and Budget (OMB) and agencies identify PPAs by reference to committee reports and budget justifications; for permanent appropriations, OMB and agencies identify PPAs by the program and financing schedules that the President provides in the "Detailed Budget Estimates" in the budget submission for the relevant fiscal year. Program activity structures are intended to provide a meaningful representation of the operations financed by a specific budget account— usually by project, activity, or organization.

PROJECTIONS

Estimates of budget authority, outlays, receipts, or other budget amounts extending several years into the future. Projections are generally intended to indicate the budgetary implications of existing or proposed programs and legislation. Projections may include alternative program and policy strategies and ranges of possible budget amounts. Projections are not firm estimates of what will occur in future years, nor are they intended to be recommendations for future budget decisions.

The statutory basis for preparing and submitting projections is spelled out (1) for the President in section 201(a) of the Budget and Accounting Act (31 U.S.C. § 1105) and (2) for Congress and the Congressional Budget Office (CBO) in sections 202, 308, and 402 of the Congressional Budget and Impoundment Control Act (2 U.S.C. §§ 601, 639, and 653). (*See also* Baseline; Budget Estimates; Multiyear Budget Planning.)

PROPRIETARY ACCOUNTING

Involves federal entities recording and accumulating financial information on transactions and balances for purposes of reporting both internally to management and externally in an entity's financial statements. "Proprietary accounting" is also referred to as "financial accounting" and is usually based on generally accepted accounting principles (GAAP), which follow established conventions, such as the recognition of the depreciation of capital assets over time as expenses, instead of recognition on the basis of strict association with the obligation or expenditure of appropriated funds. Most federal entities are subject to proprietary accounting standards promulgated through the Federal Accounting Standards Advisory Board (FASAB). (For a discussion of the methods for tracking funds in the federal government, *see* app. III. *See also* Federal Accounting Standards Advisory Board.)

PROPRIETARY ACCOUNTS

See under Standard General Ledger (SGL) Chart of Accounts.

PUBLIC-PRIVATE PARTNERSHIP

An arrangement between a public agency (federal, state, or local) and a for-profit corporation. Each sector (public and private) contributes skills and assets in delivering a service or facility for the use of the general public or the parties to the partnership.

R

REAL DOLLAR (ECONOMICS TERM)

A dollar value adjusted to remove the effects of inflation by dividing the nominal value (also called the current dollar value) by the appropriate price index. The resulting amount can be labeled real or inflation adjusted. Real dollar values can reflect a measure of purchasing power, such as real income, or a measure of quantity, such as real GDP. Real dollar is frequently called constant dollar when referring to measures of purchasing power.

REAL ECONOMIC GROWTH (ECONOMICS TERM)

The increase in GDP, adjusted for inflation.

REAL INTEREST RATE

A measure of an interest rate adjusted to remove the effects of expected general inflation.

REAL MEASURES (ECONOMICS TERM)

Measures of interest rates and prices for specific commodities adjusted to remove the effects of general inflation (i.e., real interest rates and real prices).

REAPPORTIONMENT

A revision of a previous apportionment of budgetary resources for an appropriation or fund account. The Office of Management and Budget (OMB) reapportions just as it apportions. Agencies usually submit requests for reapportionment to OMB as soon as a change becomes necessary due to changes in amounts available, program requirements, or cost factors. For exceptions, see OMB Circular No. A-11, sec. 120. This approved revision would ordinarily cover the same period, project, or activity covered in the original apportionment. (*See also* Allotment; Apportionment.)

REAUTHORIZATION

Legislation that renews an expiring or expired authorization that was in effect for a fixed period, with or without substantive change. (*See also* Authorizing Legislation.)

RECEIPTS

See under Governmental Receipts *under* Collections.

RECESSION (ECONOMICS TERM)

A pervasive, substantial decline in overall business activity that is of at least several months' duration. The National Bureau of Economic Research identifies recessions on the basis of several indicators. As a rule of thumb, recessions are commonly identified by a decline in real GDP for at least two consecutive quarters.

RECONCILIATION

A process Congress uses to reconcile amounts determined by tax, spending, credit, and debt legislation for a given fiscal year with levels set in the concurrent resolution on the budget for the year. Section 310 of the Congressional Budget and Impoundment Control Act of 1974 (2 U.S.C. §

641) provides that the resolution may direct committees to determine and recommend changes to laws and pending legislation as required to conform to the resolution's totals for budget authority, revenues, and the public debt. Such changes are incorporated into either a reconciliation resolution or a reconciliation bill. (*See also* Concurrent Resolution on the Budget; Congressional Budget Act.)

RECONCILIATION BILL

A bill reported pursuant to reconciliation instructions in a congressional budget resolution proposing changes in laws that if enacted, would achieve the budgetary goals set forth in the budget resolution. (*See also* Congressional Budget Act.)

RECONCILIATION INSTRUCTION

A provision in a concurrent budget resolution directing one or more committees to report (or submit to the House and Senate Budget Committees) legislation changing existing laws or pending legislation in order to bring spending, revenues, or debt limit into conformity with the budget resolution. The instructions specify the committees to which they apply, indicate the appropriate total dollar changes to be achieved, and usually provide a deadline by which the legislation is to be reported or submitted.

RECONCILIATION RESOLUTION

A concurrent resolution (i.e., a resolution that the President does not sign) reported pursuant to reconciliation instructions in a congressional budget resolution directing the Clerk of the House of Representatives or the Secretary of the Senate to make specified changes in bills and joint resolutions that have not been enrolled to bring direct spending or revenue laws into conformity with the budget resolution.

REDUCTION

Cancellation of the availability of budgetary resources previously provided by law before the authority would otherwise lapse. Reductions can be account specific and across-the-board. (*See also* Rescission; Sequestration.)

REFUNDS

Either (1) the return of money that the government improperly collected or collected in excess of the amount owed (for example, refund is money owed to taxpayers by the government when their total tax payments are greater than their total tax) or (2) money returned as an appropriation by outside sources for payments that the government made in error, overpayments, or adjustment for previous amounts disbursed. (*See also* *under* Offsetting Collections *under* Collections.)

REIMBURSEMENT

A sum (1) that is received by an agency as a payment for commodities sold or services furnished either to the public or to another government account and (2) that is authorized by law to be credited directly to specific appropriation and fund accounts. Reimbursements between two accounts for goods or services are usually expenditure transactions/transfers.

Anticipated reimbursements are, in the case of transactions with the public, estimated collections of expected advances to be received or expected reimbursements to be earned. In transactions between government accounts, anticipated reimbursements consist of orders expected to be received for which no orders have been accepted. Agencies cannot obligate against anticipated reimbursements without specific statutory authority. (*See also* Offsetting Collections *under* Collections; Unfilled Customer Orders.)

REOBLIGATION

Obligation of deobligated funds for a different authorized use. (*See also* Deobligation.)

REPROGRAMMING

Shifting funds within an appropriation or fund account to use them for purposes other than those contemplated at the time of appropriation; it is the shifting of funds from one object class to another within an appropriation or from one program activity to another. While a transfer of funds involves shifting funds from one account to another, reprogramming involves shifting funds within an account. (For a distinction, *see* Transfer.)

Generally agencies may shift funds within an appropriation or fund account as part of their duty to manage their funds. Unlike transfers, agencies may reprogram without additional statutory authority. Nevertheless, reprogramming often involves some form of notification to the congressional appropriations committees, authorizing committees, or both. Sometimes committee oversight of reprogramming actions is prescribed by statute and requires formal notification of one or more committees before a reprogramming action may be implemented.

RESCISSION

Legislation enacted by Congress that cancels the availability of budget authority previously enacted before the authority would otherwise expire.

The Impoundment Control Act of 1974 (2 U.S.C. § 683) provides for the President to propose rescissions whenever the President determines that all or part of any budget authority will not be needed to carry out the full objectives or scope of programs for which the authority was provided. Rescissions of budget authority may be proposed for fiscal policy or other reasons.

All funds proposed for rescission must be reported to Congress in a special message. Amounts proposed for rescission may be withheld for up to 45 calendar days of continuous session while Congress considers the proposals. If both houses have not completed action on a rescission bill rescinding all or part of the amount proposed by the President for rescission in his special message within 45 calendar days of continuous session, any funds being withheld must be made available for obligation. Congress may also initiate rescissions. Such congressional action occurs for various reasons, including changing priorities, program terminations, excessive unobligated balances, offsets, and program slippage. (*See also*

Apportionment; Budgetary Reserves; Deferral of Budget Authority; Impoundment; Reduction; Rescission Bill *under* Rescission.)

Enhanced Rescission

Legislative initiatives, proposed over the years, that would allow the President to withhold funds from obligation upon proposing a rescission and to continue withholding the funds unless and until Congress acts to disapprove the presidential proposal to rescind funds. The President could then veto the disapproval bill, forcing each house to muster a two-thirds majority to override the veto. This would be a reversal of current Impoundment Control Act procedures that require funds proposed for rescission to be released unless Congress approves, by law, all or part of the amount proposed to be rescinded by the President. In 1996, Congress enacted a form of enhanced rescission authority in the Line Item Veto Act, which authorized the President, after signing a bill into law, to cancel in whole any dollar amount of discretionary budget authority, any item of new direct spending, or any limited tax benefit if the President made certain determinations. The act provided that the cancellation was effective unless Congress enacted a disapproval bill into law to void the cancellation. In 1998, the United States Supreme Court in *Clinton v. City of New York*, 524 U.S. 417 (1998), held that the Line Item Veto Act violated the Presentment Clause, Article 1, Section 7, of the U.S. Constitution. (*See also* Impoundment; Line Item Veto; Rescission.)

Expedited Rescission

Legislative proposals designed to ensure rapid and formal congressional consideration of rescissions proposed by the President. An essential element of an expedited rescission procedure is a prompt up-or-down vote in Congress on the President's proposals to reduce enacted spending authority. This would prevent rescissions from being enacted solely due to absence of action. While such legislation has been proposed at various times in the past, Congress has not enacted expedited rescission procedures. (*See also* Impoundment; Line Item Veto; Rescission.)

Rescission Bill

A bill or joint resolution to cancel, in whole or in part, budget authority previously enacted by law. Rescissions proposed by the President must be transmitted in a special message to Congress. Under section 1012 of the Impoundment Control Act of 1974 (2 U.S.C. § 683), unless both houses of Congress complete action on a rescission bill within 45 calendar days of continuous session after receipt of the proposal, the budget authority must be made available for obligation. (*See also* Rescission.)

RESULTS-BASED BUDGETING

See under Performance Budgeting.

REVENUE

Either of the following:

(1) As used in the congressional budget process, a synonym for governmental receipts. Revenues result from amounts that result from the government's exercise of its sovereign power to tax or otherwise compel payment or from gifts to the government. Article I, Section 7, of the U.S. Constitution requires that revenue bills originate in the House of Representatives.

(2) As used in federal proprietary accounting, an inflow of resources that the government demands, earns, or receives by donation. Revenue comes from two sources: exchange transactions and nonexchange transactions. Exchange revenues arise when a government entity provides goods and services to the public or to another government entity for a price. Another term for exchange revenue is "earned revenue." Nonexchange revenues arise primarily from exercise of the government's power to demand payments from the public (e.g., taxes, duties, fines, and penalties) but also include donations. The term "revenue" does not encompass all financing sources of government reporting entities, such as most of the appropriations they receive. Revenues result from (1) services performed by the federal government and (2) goods and other property delivered to purchasers. (*See also* Collections.)

REVOLVING FUND

A fund established by Congress to finance a cycle of businesslike operations through amounts received by the fund. A revolving fund charges for the sale of products or services and uses the proceeds to finance its spending, usually on a self-sustaining basis. Instead of recording the collections in receipt accounts, the budget records the collections and the outlays of revolving funds in the same account. A revolving fund is a form of permanent appropriation. (*See also* Account.)

ROLLOVER

Instead of paying off a loan when due, the principal and sometimes accrued interest outstanding of a borrower is refinanced (rolled over) as a new loan with a new maturity date. (*See also* Federal Credit.)

S

SCOREKEEPING

The process of estimating the budgetary effects of pending legislation and comparing them to a baseline, such as a budget resolution, or to any limits that may be set in law. Scorekeeping tracks data such as budget authority, receipts, outlays, the surplus or deficit, and the public debt limit. The process allows Congress to compare the cost of proposed budget policy changes to existing law and to enforce spending and revenue levels agreed upon in the budget resolution. Budget Committees and the Congressional Budget Office (CBO) score legislation in relation to the levels set by Congress in concurrent budget resolutions.

SCOREKEEPING RULES

Guidelines established for use by the Office of Management and Budget (OMB), the Congressional Budget Office (CBO), and the Committees on Budget and Appropriations in the House of Representatives and the Senate in measuring compliance with the Balanced Budget and Emergency Deficit

Control Act, as amended by the Budget Enforcement Act (BEA), and with the congressional budget process. Though the enforcement mechanisms of BEA expired, or became ineffective, at the end of fiscal year 2002, OMB continues to use the same scorekeeping rules developed for use with BEA for purposes of budget execution. Scorekeepers (OMB, CBO, and budget committees) have an ongoing dialogue and may revise rules, as required.

SCORING

See under Scorekeeping.

SEASONAL RATE

The average commitments, obligations, and expenses of 1 or more of the last 5 fiscal years used to determine funding under a continuing resolution. (*See also* Continuing Appropriation/Continuing Resolution; Current Rate.)

SEIGNIORAGE

The difference between the face value of minted circulating coins and the cost of their production, including the cost of metal used in the minting and the cost of transporting the coins to Federal Reserve Banks for distribution to the public. Seigniorage reflects an increase in the value of government assets when coinage metal is converted to a coin whose face value is higher than the cost of the metal. Seigniorage arises from the government's exercise of its monetary powers. In contrast to receipts from the public, seigniorage involves no corresponding payment by another party. For budget reporting purposes, seigniorage is excluded from receipts and treated as a means of financing a deficit—other than borrowing from the public—or as a supplementary amount that can be applied to reduce debt or to increase the Treasury's cash. The budget includes an estimate of receipts (offsetting collections) equal to the cost of manufacturing and distributing circulating coins, including a charge for capital. (*See also* Means of Financing.)

SEPARATE ENROLLMENT

A procedure that would require that once an appropriation bill is passed by Congress, each provision of funding would be separately enrolled as a discrete "bill." An enrolled bill is the final, official copy of a bill or joint resolution that both houses have passed in identical form to present to the President for signature. Each separately enrolled provision would be presented independently to the President for signature, allowing the veto of some "bills" with spending provisions to which the President objects while allowing signing the others. While such legislation has been proposed at various times in the past as a way of providing the President with something like a line item veto, Congress has not enacted separate enrollment procedures. (*See also* Impoundment; Line Item Veto; Rescission.)

SEQUESTER

See under Sequestration.

SEQUESTRATION (BUDGET ENFORCEMENT ACT TERM)

Under Budget Enforcement Act (BEA) provisions, which expired in 2002, the cancellation of budgetary resources provided by discretionary appropriations or direct spending laws. New budget authority, unobligated balances, direct spending authority, and obligation limitations were "sequestrable" resources; that is, they were subject to reduction or cancellation under a presidential sequester order. (*See also* Budgetary Resources; Entitlement Authority; Gramm-Rudman-Hollings; Impoundment; Rescission.)

SPECIAL FUND ACCOUNTS

See under Federal Fund Accounts *under* Accounts in the President's Budget.

SPENDING CAPS

Overall limits on discretionary spending, which were originally set in the Budget Enforcement Act (BEA) and the enforcement of which expired at the end of fiscal year 2002. Congress, however, continues to set limits on discretionary spending, typically in concurrent budget resolutions, which are enforceable during the congressional budget process. (*See also* Discretionary; Concurrent Resolution on the Budget.)

SPENDING COMMITTEE

A standing committee of the House or Senate with jurisdiction over legislation permitting the obligation of funds. The House and Senate Appropriations Committees are spending committees for discretionary programs. For other programs, the authorizing legislation itself permits the obligation of funds (backdoor authority). In that case, the authorizing committees are the spending committees. (*See also* Authorizing Committee; Backdoor Authority/Backdoor Spending.)

SPENDOUT RATE/OUTLAY RATE

The rate at which budget authority becomes outlays in a fiscal year. It is usually presented as an annual percentage.

STANDARD GENERAL LEDGER (SGL) CHART OF ACCOUNTS

A chart of accounts (and technical guidance) established to support the consistent recording of financial events as well as the preparation of standard external reports required by the Office of Management and Budget (OMB) and the Department of the Treasury. Agencies are required by law (31 U.S.C. § 3512) to "implement and maintain financial management systems that comply substantially with," among other things, the *Standard General Ledger*. It contains two complete and separate, but integrated, self-balancing sets of accounts—budgetary and proprietary. Budgetary accounts are used to recognize and track budget approval and execution, whereas proprietary accounts are used to recognize and track assets, liabilities, revenues, and expenses. The *Standard General Ledger* is reproduced in the *Treasury Financial Manual* "Standard General Ledger Supplement," available at www.fms.treas.gov/ussgl/index.html. OMB policies regarding the *Standard General Ledger* are in OMB Circular No. A-127.

STATEMENT OF FEDERAL FINANCIAL ACCOUNTING STANDARDS (SFFAS)

See under Federal Accounting Standards Advisory Board.

STRUCTURAL/STANDARDIZED BUDGET SURPLUS/DEFICIT (ECONOMICS TERM)

A concept adjusting the surplus/deficit for the effects of the business cycle and other temporary factors such as sales and spectrum auctions.

STRUCTURAL SURPLUS/DEFICIT (ECONOMICS TERM)

See under Cyclically Adjusted Surplus or Deficit.

SUBCOMMITTEE ALLOCATION

As required by section 302(b) of the Congressional Budget and Impoundment Control Act of 1974 (2 U.S.C. § 633(b)), the distribution of spending authority and outlays by the appropriations committees of each house of Congress to their relevant appropriations subcommittees of jurisdiction based on the levels contained in the concurrent resolution on the budget.

SUBFUNCTION

A subdivision of a budget function. For example, health care services and health research are subfunctions of the health budget function. (For a presentation of the budget in terms of subfunctions, *see* app. IV. *See also* Functional Classification.)

SUBSIDY

Generally, a payment or benefit made by the federal government where the benefit exceeds the cost to the beneficiary. Subsidies are designed to support the conduct of an economic enterprise or activity, such as ship operations. They may also refer to (1) provisions in the tax laws for certain tax expenditures and (2) the provision of loans, goods, and services to the public at prices lower than market value. These include interest subsidies.

Under credit reform, subsidy means the estimated long-term cost to the government of a direct loan or loan guarantee, calculated on a net present value basis over the life of the loan, excluding administrative costs and any incidental effects on governmental receipts or outlays. (*See also* Credit Reform *and* Credit Subsidy Cost *under* Federal Credit; Tax Expenditure.)

SUBSIDY COST

See under Credit Subsidy Cost *under* Federal Credit.

SUPPLEMENTAL APPROPRIATION

An act appropriating funds in addition to those already enacted in an annual appropriation act. Supplemental appropriations provide additional budget authority usually in cases where the need for funds is too urgent to be postponed until enactment of the regular appropriation bill. Supplementals may sometimes include items not appropriated in the regular bills for lack of timely authorizations.

SURPLUS

Budget Surplus

The amount by which the government's budget receipts exceed its budget outlays for a given period, usually a fiscal year. Sometimes a deficit is called a negative surplus and is shown in parentheses in budget tables.

Unified Surplus/Total Surplus

Used interchangeably to refer to the amount by which the sum of the government's on-budget and off-budget receipts exceed the sum of its on-budget and off-budget outlays for a given period, usually a fiscal year. (*See also* Unified Deficit/Total Deficit *under* Deficit.)

T

TAX

A sum that legislation imposes upon persons (broadly defined to include individuals, trusts, estates, partnerships, associations, companies, and corporations), property, or activities to pay for government operations. The power to impose and collect federal taxes is given to Congress in Article I, Section 8, of the U.S. Constitution. Collections that arise from the sovereign powers of the federal government constitute the bulk of governmental receipts, which are compared with budget outlays in calculating the budget surplus or deficit. (*See also* Government Receipts *under* Collections; Revenue.)

TAX CREDIT

An amount that offsets or reduces tax liability. When the allowable tax credit amount exceeds the tax liability and the difference is paid to the taxpayer, the credit is considered refundable and is considered an increase in outlays in the federal budget. Otherwise, the difference can be (1) allowed as a carryforward against future tax liability, (2) allowed as a carryback against taxes paid, or (3) lost as a tax benefit. (*See also* Tax Expenditure.)

TAX DEDUCTION

An amount that is subtracted from the tax base before tax liability is calculated.

TAX EXPENDITURE

A revenue loss attributable to a provision of the federal tax laws that (1) allows a special exclusion, exemption, or deduction from gross income or (2) provides a special credit, preferential tax rate, or deferral of tax liability. Tax expenditures are subsidies provided through the tax system. Rather than transferring funds from the government to the private sector, the U.S. government forgoes some of the receipts that it would have collected, and the beneficiary taxpayers pay lower taxes than they would have had to pay. The Congressional Budget Act requires that a list of "tax expenditures" be included in the President's budget. Examples include tax expenditures for child care and the exclusion of fringe benefits, such as employer-provided health insurance, from taxation.

TECHNICAL AND ECONOMIC ASSUMPTIONS

Assumptions about factors affecting estimations of future outlays and receipts that are not a direct function of legislation. Economic assumptions involve such factors as the future inflation and interest rates. Technical assumptions involve all other nonpolicy factors. For example, in the Medicare program, estimations regarding demography, hospitalization versus outpatient treatment, and morbidity all affect estimations of future outlays.

302(A) ALLOCATION

See under Committee Allocation.

302(B) ALLOCATION

See under Subcommittee Allocation.

TRANSFER

Shifting of all or part of the budget authority in one appropriation or fund account to another. Agencies may transfer budget authority only as specifically authorized by law. For accounting purposes, the nature of the transfer determines whether the transaction is treated as an expenditure or a nonexpenditure transfer. (*See also* Allocation. For a distinction, *see* Reprogramming.)

Expenditure Transfer

For accounting and reporting purposes, a transaction between appropriation and fund accounts, which represents payments, repayments, or receipts for goods or services furnished or to be furnished.

Where the purpose is to purchase goods or services or otherwise benefit the transferring account, an expenditure transfer/transaction is recorded as an obligation/outlay in the transferring account and an offsetting collection in the receiving account.

If the receiving account is a general fund appropriation account or a revolving fund account, the offsetting collection is credited to the appropriation or fund account. If the receiving account is a special fund or trust account, the offsetting collection is usually credited to a receipt account of the fund.

All transfers between federal funds (general, special, and nontrust revolving funds) and trust funds are also treated as expenditure transfers.

Nonexpenditure Transfer

For accounting and reporting purposes, a transaction between appropriation and fund accounts that does not represent payments for goods and services received or to be received but rather serves only to adjust the amounts available in the accounts for making payments. However, transactions between budget accounts and deposit funds will always be treated as expenditure transactions since the deposit funds are outside the budget. Nonexpenditure transfers also include allocations. These transfers may not be recorded as obligations or outlays of the transferring accounts or as reimbursements or receipts of the receiving accounts. For example, the transfer of budget authority from one account to another to absorb the cost of a federal pay raise is a nonexpenditure transfer. (*See* Allocation; *see also* Transfer Appropriation (Allocation) Accounts *under* Accounts for Purposes Other Than Budget Presentation.)

TRANSFER AUTHORITY

Statutory authority provided by Congress to transfer budget authority from one appropriation or fund account to another.

TRANSFER PAYMENT (ECONOMICS TERM)

A payment made for which no current or future goods or services are required in return. Government transfer payments include Social Security benefits, unemployment insurance benefits, and welfare payments. Taxes are considered transfer payments. Governments also receive transfer payments in the form of fees, fines, and donations from businesses and persons. (*See also* National Income and Product Accounts.)

TREASURY SECURITY

A debt instrument of the U.S. Treasury issued to finance the operations of the government or refinance the government's debt.

Treasury Bill

The shortest term federal debt instrument or security. Treasury bills mature within 1 year after the date of issue.

Treasury Bond

A federal debt instrument with a maturity of more than 10 years.

Treasury Note

A federal debt instrument with a maturity of at least 1 year but not more than 10 years.

TRUST FUND ACCOUNTS

See under Account in the President's Budget.

U

UNCOLLECTED CUSTOMER PAYMENTS FROM FEDERAL SOURCES

Orders on hand from other federal government accounts that are recorded as valid obligations of the ordering account and for which funds or noncash resources have not yet been collected. The amount represents both accounts receivable from federal sources and unpaid, unfilled orders from federal sources.

UNDELIVERED ORDERS

The value of goods and services ordered and obligated that have not been received. This amount includes any orders for which advance payment has been made but for which delivery or performance has not yet occurred. (*See also* Advance Payments; Unliquidated Obligations.)

UNDISTRIBUTED OFFSETTING RECEIPTS

Offsetting receipts that are deducted from totals for the government as a whole rather than from a single agency or subfunction in order to avoid distortion of agency or subfunction totals. Offsetting receipts that are undistributed in both agency and functional tables are the collections of employer share of employee retirement payments, rents, and royalties on the Outer Continental Shelf, and the sales of major assets.

Interest received by trust funds is undistributed offsetting receipts in the agency tables, but is distributed by function (i.e., subfunction 950 in functional tables).

UNEMPLOYMENT RATE (ECONOMICS TERM)

As defined by the Bureau of Labor Statistics (BLS), the number of people who do not have jobs but have actively looked for work in the prior 4 weeks and are currently available for work, expressed as a percentage of the civilian labor force.

UNFILLED CUSTOMER ORDERS

The dollar amount of orders accepted from other accounts within the government for goods and services to be furnished on a reimbursable basis. In the case of transactions with the public, these orders are amounts advanced or collected for which the account or fund has not yet performed the service or incurred its own obligations for that purpose. (*See also* Reimbursements *under* Offsetting Collections *under* Collections.)

UNFUNDED MANDATE

Federal statutes and regulations that require state, local, or tribal governments or the private sector to expend resources to achieve legislative goals without being provided federal funding to cover the costs.

The Unfunded Mandates Reform Act of 1995, Pub. L. No. 104-4 (2 U.S.C. §§ 658–658g), generally defines intergovernmental and private sector mandates as "any provision in legislation, statute, or regulation that imposes an enforceable duty" but excludes "conditions of federal assistance" and "duties that arise from participation in a voluntary federal program," among others. The Congressional Budget Office (CBO) is required to determine whether the costs to the states or private sector of a mandate in legislation reported from a congressional committee exceeds certain statutory thresholds. This determination is included in the cost estimate provided to Congress on that legislation. The act also contains procedures for congressional consideration of proposed legislation that contains mandates whose costs are estimated to be over the thresholds unless the legislation also provides funding to cover those costs.

UNIFIED BUDGET

Under budget concepts set forth in the *Report of the President's Commission on Budget Concepts*, a comprehensive budget in which receipts and outlays from federal and trust funds are consolidated. When these fund groups are consolidated to display budget totals, transactions that are outlays of one fund group for payment to the other fund group (that is, interfund transactions) are deducted to avoid double counting. The unified budget should, as conceived by the President's Commission, take in the full range of federal activities. By law, budget authority, outlays, and receipts of off-budget programs (currently only the Postal Service and Social Security) are excluded from the current budget, but data relating to off-budget programs are displayed in the budget documents. However, the most prominent total in the budget is the unified total, which is the sum of the on- and off-budget totals. (*See also* Nonbudgetary; Off-Budget; On-Budget.)

UNLIQUIDATED OBLIGATIONS

The amount of outstanding obligations or liabilities. (*See also* Obligation; Undelivered Orders.)

USER FEE/USER CHARGE

A fee assessed to users for goods or services provided by the federal government. User fees generally apply to federal programs or activities that provide special benefits to identifiable recipients above and beyond what is normally available to the public. User fees are normally related to the cost of the goods or services provided. Once collected, they must be deposited into the general fund of the Treasury, unless the agency has specific authority to deposit the fees into a special fund of the Treasury. An agency may not obligate against fees collected without specific statutory authority. An example of a user fee is a fee for entering a national park.

From an economic point of view, user fees may also be collected through a tax such as an excise tax. Since these collections result from the government's sovereign powers, the proceeds are recorded as governmental receipts, not as offsetting receipts or offsetting collections.

In the narrow budgetary sense, a toll for the use of a highway is considered a user fee because it is related to the specific use of a particular section of highway. Such a fee would be counted as an offsetting receipt or collection and might be available for use by the agency. Alternatively, highway excise taxes on gasoline are considered a form of user charge in the economic sense, but since the tax must be paid regardless of how the gasoline is used and since it is not directly linked with the provision of the specific service, it is considered a tax and is recorded as a governmental receipt in the budget. (*See also* Offsetting Collections *under* Collections; Tax.)

V

VIEWS AND ESTIMATES REPORT

A report that the Congressional Budget Act of 1974 requires each House and Senate committee with jurisdiction over federal programs to submit to its respective budget committees each year within 6 weeks of the submission of the President's budget, in advance of the House and Senate Budget Committees' drafting of a concurrent resolution on the budget. Each report contains a committee's comments or recommendations on budgetary matters within its jurisdiction. (*See also* Concurrent Resolution on the Budget.)

W

WARRANT

An official document that the Secretary of the Treasury issues upon enactment of an appropriation that establishes the amount of moneys authorized to be withdrawn from the central accounts that the Department of the Treasury maintains. Warrants for currently unavailable special and trust fund receipts are issued when requirements for their availability have been met. (For a discussion of availability, *see* Availability for New Obligations *under* Budget Authority.)

WHOLLY-OWNED GOVERNMENT CORPORATION

An enterprise or business activity designated by the Government Corporation Control Act of 1945 (31 U.S.C. § 9101) or some other statute as a wholly-owned government corporation. Each such corporation is required to submit an annual business-type statement to the Office of Management and Budget (OMB). Wholly-owned government corporations are audited by Government Accountability Office (GAO) as required by the Government Corporation Control Act, as amended (31 U.S.C. § 9105), and other laws. The Pension Benefit Guaranty Corporation is an example of a wholly-owned government corporation. Budget concepts call for any corporation that is wholly owned by the government to be included on-budget. (For distinctions, *see* Government-Sponsored Enterprise; Mixed-Ownership Government Corporation; Off-Budget.)

WORKING CAPITAL FUND

A type of intragovernmental revolving fund that operates as a self-supporting entity that conducts a regular cycle of businesslike activities. These funds function entirely from the fees charged for the services they provide consistent with their statutory authority. (*See also* Intragovernmental Revolving Fund Account *under* Intragovernmental Fund Accounts *under* Federal Fund Accounts *under* Account in the President's Budget.)

Chapter 2

APPENDIX I

United States Government Accountability Office

OVERVIEW OF THE DEVELOPMENT AND APENDIXES EXECUTION OF THE FEDERAL BUDGET

The United States Constitution gives Congress the power to levy taxes, to finance government operations through appropriations, and to prescribe the conditions governing the use of those appropriations. This power is referred to as the congressional "power of the purse." The power derives from various provisions of the Constitution,[1] particularly article I, section 9, clause 7, which provides that "No money shall be drawn from the Treasury, but in Consequence of Appropriations made by Law; and a regular Statement and Account of the Receipts and Expenditures of all public Money shall be published from time to time."

Thus an agency may not draw money out of the Treasury to fund agency operations unless Congress has appropriated the money to the agency. At its

---

[1] Some examples of other provisions in the Constitution relating to the spending and control of funds are those to lay and collect taxes, duties, imposts, and excises; to borrow money on the credit of the United States; to "pay the Debts and provide for the common Defence and general Welfare of the United States;" and to "make all Laws which shall be necessary and proper for carrying into Execution the foregoing Powers [listed in art. I, § 8], and all other Powers vested by this Constitution in the Government of the United States, or in any Department or Officer thereof." These provisions are all found in article I, section 8, of the Constitution.

most basic level, this means that it is up to Congress to decide whether to provide funds for a particular program or activity and to fix the level of that funding. Although the Constitution does not provide detailed instructions on how Congress is to do so, Congress has and continues to implement its power of the purse in two ways: through the enactment of laws that raise revenue and appropriate funds, including annual appropriations acts, and through the enactment of "fiscal statutes" that control and manage federal revenue and appropriations (one such fiscal statute, the Antideficiency Act, is explained in detail in phase 3).[2]

A "budget," in customary usage, is a plan for managing funds, setting levels of spending, and financing that spending. For purposes of this overview, however, the "federal budget" is used more broadly to include not only the planning through the federal budget process, but also the end result of that plan after the fiscal effect of spending and revenue laws in effect for any given fiscal year are calculated. Those laws consist of permanent laws enacted in prior years, including any permanent appropriations, and the appropriations acts enacted for that fiscal year.

Beginning in 1921, Congress enacted laws that provide a framework of procedures for coordinating and planning for federal spending and revenues. The Budget and Accounting Act of 1921 requires the President to submit an annual budget proposal to Congress and established the Office of Management and Budget (OMB) and the Government Accountability Office (GAO) (formerly, the General Accounting Office). In 1974, Congress enacted the Congressional Budget and Impoundment Control Act, which provides for the adoption of a budget resolution and established the House and Senate Budget Committees and the Congressional Budget Office (CBO). These laws overlay the existing processes by which Congress enacts and the President signs into law spending and revenue measures and have come to be known, collectively, as the federal budget process.

The federal budget process provides the means for the federal government to make informed decisions between competing national needs and policies, to determine priorities, to allocate resources to those priorities, and to ensure the laws are executed according to those priorities. The federal budget process can be broken down into four phases: budget formulation, the congressional budget process (during which Congress adopts its budget and enacts laws appropriating funds for the fiscal year), budget execution and

---

[2] The budget process and the financial management process (i.e., ensuring that federal financial management systems provide accurate, reliable, and timely financial management information to the government's managers, the President, and Congress) are closely related.

control, and audit and evaluation. The discussion that follows describes in detail the four phases of the federal budget process.

PHASE 1: EXECUTIVE BUDGET FORMULATION

The federal government begins to assemble an annual federal budget in a long administrative process of budget preparation and review. This process may well take place several years before the budget for a particular fiscal year is ready to be submitted to Congress. The primary participants in the process at this stage are the agencies and individual organizational units, which review current operations, program objectives, and future plans, and OMB, the office within the Executive Office of the President charged with broad oversight, supervision, and responsibility for coordinating and formulating a consolidated budget submission. (See fig. 1 in app. II.)

By the first Monday in February, the President submits a budget request to Congress for the fiscal year starting on the following October 1 (i.e., in February 2005 the President submitted the budget request for fiscal year 2006, which runs from October 1, 2005, through September 30, 2006). However, preparation of this particular budget request began about 10 months before it was submitted to Congress. For example, for the fiscal year 2006 budget request, transmitted to Congress in February 2005, the budget process began in the spring of 2004. Thus, federal agencies must deal concurrently with 3 fiscal years: (1) the current year, that is, the fiscal year in progress; (2) the coming fiscal year beginning October 1, for which they are seeking funds (for purposes of formulation of the President's budget request, this fiscal year is known as the budget year); and (3) the following fiscal year, for which they are preparing information and requests. OMB Circular No. A-11, *Preparation, Submission, and Execution of the Budget* (revised annually), provides detailed guidance to executive departments and establishments on preparing budget submissions. The President's budget, which is the sole single document with budget information for the entire government, contains

- a record of actual receipts and spending levels for the fiscal year just completed;
- a record of current-year estimated receipts and spending; and
- estimated receipts and spending for the upcoming fiscal year and 9 years beyond, as proposed by the President.

Executive budget formulation, based upon proposals, evaluations, and policy decisions, begins in agencies' organizational units. During executive budget formulation, federal agencies receive revenue estimates and economic projections from the Department of the Treasury (Treasury), the Council of Economic Advisers (CEA), and OMB.

Executive Budget Formulation Timetable

Spring–Summer: OMB Establishes Policy for the Next Budget Request

During this period, OMB and the executive branch agencies discuss budget issues and options. OMB works with the agencies to identify major issues for the upcoming budget request; to develop and analyze options for the upcoming reviews of agency spending and program requests; and to plan for the analysis of issues that will need decisions in the future. OMB issues policy directions and planning guidance to the agencies for the upcoming budget request and detailed instructions for submitting budget data and materials for the upcoming fiscal year and following 9 fiscal years.

September–October: Agencies Submit Initial Budget Request Materials

By law, the President's budget request must include information on all agencies of all three branches of the federal government.[3] Executive branch departments, agencies that are subject to executive branch review, and the District of Columbia must submit their budget requests and other initial materials to OMB typically the first Monday after Labor Day of the year prior to the start of the year that the budget request covers (i.e., September 8, 2004, for fiscal year 2006, which started October 1, 2005). Agencies not subject to executive branch review (e.g., the Federal Reserve Board) and the legislative and judicial branches are required to submit their budget materials in fall of the year prior to the year that the budget requests cover (e.g., in October 2004 for fiscal year 2006).[4]

---

[3] 31 U.S.C. § 1105.

[4] The budget requests for the legislative branch and the judicial branch and its related agencies must be submitted to OMB in late fall of each year and included in the President's budget request without change. The budget requests of several executive branch agencies are not subject to review by OMB. See OMB Circular No. A-11, sec. 25.1. Information on all three branches of government is

October–December: OMB Performs Review and Makes Passback Decisions

OMB staff representatives conduct the fall review. OMB has informal discussions with agencies about their budget proposals in light of presidential priorities, program performance, and any budget constraints. OMB examiners prepare issues for the Director's review. The Director briefs the President and senior advisors on proposed budget policies and recommends a complete set of budget proposals after a review of all agency requests. The President considers the estimates and makes his decisions on broad policies. In late November, OMB passes back budget decisions to the agencies on their budget requests, the so-called passback. These decisions may involve, among other things, funding levels, program policy changes, and personnel ceilings. The agencies may appeal decisions with which they disagree. If OMB and an agency cannot reach agreement, the issue may be taken to the President.

Final budget decisions will also reflect proposals for management and program-delivery improvements resulting from agency and OMB reviews during the executive budget formulation process. OMB not only assists in making individual budget decisions, it also tracks the result of these decisions. OMB calculates the effect of budget decisions on receipts, budget authority, and outlays. Once final decisions on the budget requests are reached, agencies revise their budget submissions to conform to these decisions. These final estimates are transmitted to Congress in the President's budget request.

By the First Monday in February: President Submits Budget Request

In accordance with current law, the President must transmit the budget request to Congress on or before the first Monday in February.[5]

By July 15: President Submits Mid-Session Review Document to Congress

The Budget and Accounting Act of 1921, as amended, requires the President to submit to Congress on or before July 15 a supplementary budget summary that provides data to aid in evaluation of the President's budget

---

included in the President's budget request so that Congress may review one submission that covers the entire government.

[5] 31 U.S.C. § 1105(a).

request.[6] This summary, referred to as the mid-session review, includes updated presidential policy budget estimates, summary updates to the information contained in the budget submission, and budget-year baseline estimates.

PHASE 2: THE CONGRESSIONAL BUDGET PROCESS

Once the President submits his budget request, the congressional phase begins. Since the constitutional power of the purse is vested solely in Congress, the President's budget request is just that—a request. Congress, of course, may choose to adopt, modify, or ignore the President's budget proposals when adopting its budget resolution and when enacting appropriations and other laws. (See fig. 2 in app. II.)

The Congressional Budget Act establishes the following key steps in the congressional budget process.

January–February: CBO Submits Report to the Budget Committees and Congress Receives the President's Budget Request

Usually in late January, CBO submits to the Budget Committees its annual report, entitled *The Budget and Economic Outlook*. The report contains CBO's projection of federal revenue and spending for the next 10 years, based on its current economic forecast and the general assumption that existing laws and policies remain unchanged.

Congress receives the President's budget request no later than the first Monday in February. At the same time, the President transmits current services estimates to Congress. The House and Senate Budget Committees, in preparation for drafting the concurrent resolution on the budget, hold hearings to examine the President's economic assumptions and spending priorities. At the request of the Senate Appropriations Committee, CBO prepares an analysis of the President's request.

Committees Transmit the Views and Estimates Reports to Budget Committees

While the Budget Committees examine aggregate budget levels and budget functions, the other committees of Congress with jurisdiction over federal programs transmit to the Budget Committees their views and estimates on spending and revenue levels for programs under their

---

[6] 31 U.S.C. § 1106.

jurisdiction. The Budget Committees use these reports on views and estimates to develop the total revenue and spending estimates that they will propose in the concurrent budget resolution. In conjunction with these views and estimates reports, the Joint Economic Committee submits its recommendations concerning fiscal policy to the Budget Committees.

March–April: Congress Adopts a Budget Resolution

Typically, during March, the Budget Committees mark-up and report to their respective houses a budget plan in the form of a concurrent resolution on the budget. This budget resolution is drafted using the President's budget request, information from their own hearings, views and estimates reports from other committees, and CBO's reports. The budget resolution is required to set forth (for the upcoming fiscal year and for each of at least the next 4 years) the total level of new budget authority, outlays, revenues, the deficit or surplus, the public debt, and spending by functional category. The budget resolution may include reconciliation instructions to the extent necessary to meet the revenue or direct spending targets in the budget resolution.

The budget resolution is considered in each House under special procedures set forth in the Congressional Budget Act. When the Senate and House have both adopted their respective versions of the budget resolution, it is referred to a conference committee to resolve the differences between the two versions. Each chamber must then vote on the conference report. The Congressional Budget Act sets April 15 as the date by which Congress should complete action on the budget resolution; however, in practice, Congress may not meet this date.[7] For example, in 2005 Congress adopted the budget resolution for fiscal year 2006 on April 28, 2005. In 1998 (for fiscal year 1999), in 2002 (for fiscal year 2003), and in 2004 (for fiscal year 2005) Congress did not complete action on budget resolutions.[8]

---

[7] Article I, section 5, clause 2, of the Constitution reserves to each House of Congress the authority to determine the rules governing its procedures. The Budget Act contains several titles and sections that affect the internal procedures of the House and Senate enacted under this constitutional rule-making authority. Congress enacted the Budget Act with the full recognition that each House could change these rules at any time and in a manner consistent with past practice. Rule changes are usually accomplished upon adoption of either a simple resolution (for a change that affects one House) or a concurrent resolution (for changes that may affect both houses). S. Rep. No. 105-67 (revised December 1998).

[8] See Bill Heniff, Jr., *Congressional Budget Resolutions: Selected Statistics and Information Guide* (Washington, D.C.: Congressional Research Service, Jan. 25, 2005).

The joint explanatory statement accompanying a conference report on the budget resolution includes an allocation of budget authority and outlays to the Appropriations Committees (for discretionary spending) and to each authorizing committee (for direct spending) of the House and Senate. The Appropriations Committees subsequently subdivide their allocation among their subcommittees according to jurisdiction.

The concurrent resolution on the budget does not become law; it is not signed by the President. The aggregate levels of revenues, budget authority, and outlays and the committee allocations are guidelines and targets against which subsequent fiscal legislation—appropriation acts; authorizing legislation that provides budget authority; revenue acts; and, if necessary, reconciliation acts (see below)—is measured.

The Congressional Budget Act contains rules of the House and Senate that implement the priorities agreed to and set in the concurrent resolution on the budget. These rules generally prohibit the consideration of legislation that is not in compliance with the committee allocations or the revenue or spending totals in the resolution. Accordingly, if legislation is out of compliance, it is subject to a point of order and, if the point of order is sustained, Congress is precluded from further consideration of the legislation until it is brought into compliance.[9]

If changing economic circumstances or policy requirements dictate, Congress may revise its budget resolution during the fiscal year, thereby altering the spending and revenue totals.

May–September: Congress Addresses Fiscal Legislation

Reconciliation Measure

When the concurrent resolution on the budget contains reconciliation instructions, the committees must submit legislative language that changes laws in their jurisdiction to the Budget Committee of their house on the date

---

[9] In fiscal year 1994, Congress began including overall limits on discretionary spending in the budget resolution, known as spending caps or discretionary caps. Congress established these caps to manage its internal budget process, while the Budget Enforcement Act (BEA) statutory caps continued to govern for sequestration purposes. The caps were enforceable in the Senate by a point of order that prohibited the consideration of a budget resolution that exceeded the limits for that fiscal year. While the BEA limits expired at the end of fiscal year 2002, Congress continues to use the budget resolution to establish and enforce overall discretionary spending limits.

specified in the instructions. The Budget Committees may make no substantive changes to the submissions, but must report the submissions to the House or Senate as a single reconciliation bill. If, however, a reconciled committee fails to meet the numerical targets included in its reconciliation instruction, procedures exist to modify the bill on the floor so that the targets are met. (If only one committee is instructed, that committee reports its recommendations directly to the House or Senate.)

The reconciliation legislation is a unique vehicle through which Congress enforces its budget plan for revenue and direct spending set forth in the budget resolution. Both the House of Representatives and the Senate consider the reconciliation legislation reported to them from their respective Budget Committees under special rules. (The Appropriations Committees are not subject to reconciliation instructions.) Generally, in the House, the legislation is considered under a special rule, a simple resolution adopted by the House prior to consideration of the reconciliation legislation that governs the debate and the amendments that are in order. In the Senate, reconciliation legislation is considered under special procedures set forth in the Congressional Budget Act, which limits the period of debate and the types of amendments that are in order and subjects the legislation and amendments to the Byrd Rule, which prohibits "extraneous material." (See Byrd Rule for more detail.)

The differences between the two houses are typically resolved in a conference committee and the resulting legislation is passed by both houses and must be signed by the President to become law.

Appropriations and Other Fiscal Legislation

Generally, throughout this period, Congress considers revenue legislation and legislation affecting spending, including the regular appropriations acts.[10] All legislation considered by Congress that affects revenue or spending must comply with the committee allocations and the total levels of revenues and spending in the concurrent resolution on the budget.[11]

---

[10] Less than 40 percent of total budget authority is appropriated through the annual appropriations process. The remainder of the budgetary resources spent by the federal government are provided by law other than annual appropriations acts. (For further explanation, see the definitions of Backdoor Authority, Budget Authority, Direct Spending, Obligational Authority, and Outlay.)

[11] The rules of the House of Representatives also prohibit consideration of appropriations bills for expenditures not previously authorized by law. See Rule XXI, Rules of the House of Representatives. A similar, but more limited

Appropriations bills are developed by the House and Senate Appropriations Committees and their subcommittees. Each subcommittee has jurisdiction over specific federal agencies or programs and is responsible for one of the general appropriations bills.[12] The Constitution requires that all revenue (tax) bills originate in the House; by custom, the House also originates appropriations measures.

The Congressional Budget Act requires that the House and Senate Appropriations Committees subdivide the amounts allocated to them under the budget resolution among their subcommittees (Section 302(b) allocations).[13] Once the subcommittees receive their allocations, the subcommittees begin drafting their appropriations bills to fund discretionary spending programs. Proposed legislation that would cause the section 302(b) allocations to be exceeded is subject to a point of order.

CBO prepares a cost estimate on each appropriations bill, just as it provides cost estimates for any legislative measure reported by a committee of Congress. The Budget Committees use this information to determine whether the legislation complies with a committee's allocation, a subcommittee's suballocation, and the budget totals in the budget resolution.

Congress must enact these regular appropriations bills by October 1 of each year. If these regular bills are not enacted by the deadline (and they

---

provision exists in Rule XVI, Standing Rules of the Senate. (See Point of Order.) (Some agency programs or functions are reauthorized every year, while others are authorized for several years or permanently.) The effect of such rules is that an appropriation bill is subject to a point of order if it is not preceded by an authorization of appropriation.

[12] As of March 2005, the House of Representatives has 10 appropriation subcommittees: Agriculture, Rural Development, Food and Drug Administration, and Related Agencies; Defense; Energy and Water Development, and Related Agencies; Foreign Operations, Export Financing and Related Programs; Homeland Security; Interior, Environment, and Related Agencies; Labor, Health and Human Services, Education, and Related Agencies; Military Quality of Life and Veterans Affairs and Related Agencies; Science, the Departments of State, Justice, and Commerce, and Related Agencies; and Transportation, Treasury, and Housing and Urban Development, the Judiciary, and the District of Columbia. The Senate has 12 appropriation subcommittees: Agriculture, Rural Development, and Related Agencies; Commerce, Justice, and Science; Defense; District of Columbia; Energy and Water; Homeland Security; Interior and Related Agencies; Labor, Health and Human Services, Education and Related Agencies; Legislative Branch; Military Construction and Veterans Affairs; State, Foreign Operations, and Related Programs; and Transportation, Treasury, the Judiciary, Housing and Urban Development, and Related Agencies.

[13] 2 U.S.C. § 633.

usually are not), Congress must pass a continuing resolution prior to the beginning of each fiscal year to fund government operations into the next fiscal year. When an agency does not receive its new appropriation before its current appropriation expires, it must cease ongoing, regular functions that are funded with annual appropriations, except for those related to emergencies involving the safety of human life or the protection of property.

PHASE 3: BUDGET EXECUTION AND CONTROL

The body of enacted laws providing appropriations for a fiscal year becomes the government's financial plan for that fiscal year. The execution and control phase refers generally to the period during which the budget authority made available by appropriations remains available for obligation. An agency's task during this phase is to spend the money Congress has given it to carry out the objectives of its program legislation in accordance with fiscal statutes and appropriations, while at the same time beginning phase 1 for the next budget.

The Antideficiency Act is one of these fiscal statutes. It is a funds control, financial management statute, and it achieves this funds control objective through a system of apportionments, allotments, suballotments, and allocation of funds. It requires that agency heads prescribe, by regulation, a system of administrative control of funds. The system is also called the funds control system, and the regulations are called funds control regulations.

OMB is responsible for apportioning appropriated amounts to the executive branch agencies, thereby making funds in appropriation accounts (administered by Treasury) available for obligation. The apportionment is intended to achieve an effective and orderly use of available budget authority and ensure that obligations and expenditures are made at a controlled rate to reduce the need for supplemental appropriations, and prevent deficiencies from arising before the end of a fiscal year.

Once OMB apportions funds, it is the agency's responsibility to allocate the funds in accordance with its funds control system and regulations. The purpose of the funds control system and regulations is (1) to prevent overobligations and expenditures and (2) to fix accountability for obligations or expenditures. An obligation or expenditure that exceeds the amount of the appropriation, the apportionment, or the allotment violates the Antideficiency Act. For a more detailed explanation of these controls, see GAO/OGC-92-13, *Principles of Federal Appropriations Law*, volume II, second edition (available at www.gao.gov/legal.htm), and OMB Circular No. A-11, part 4, *Instructions on Budget Execution.*

Impoundment

At various times, the executive branch has refused to execute appropriations laws, that is, refused to spend money appropriated by Congress because the executive branch disagreed with the use of the funds. Under the Impoundment Control Act of 1974 whenever the President, the Director of OMB, or an agency or other federal government official does not make an appropriation or any part of an appropriation available for obligation, that official is impounding funds. The act permits the President, the Director of OMB, or an agency or other federal government official to impound funds only for certain reasons and under certain circumstances. The act also requires that impoundments be reported to Congress and the Comptroller General of the United States. The act requires the Comptroller General to monitor the performance of the executive branch in reporting proposed impoundments to Congress. For more information on impoundments, see section D.3 (Budget Execution and Control: Impoundment) in *Principles of Federal Appropriations Law,* volume I, third edition, GAO-04-261SP (available at www.gao.gov/special.pubs/redbook1.html).

PHASE 4: AUDIT AND EVALUATION

Individual agencies are responsible—through their own review and control systems—for ensuring that the obligations they incur and the resulting outlays adhere to the provisions in the authorizing and appropriations legislation as well as to other laws and regulations governing the obligation and expenditure of funds. OMB Circular No. A-11 provides extensive guidance to agencies on budget execution. In addition, a series of federal laws are aimed at controlling and improving agency financial management. The Inspector General Act of 1978, Pub. L. No. 95–452 as amended, established agency inspectors general to provide policy direction for and to conduct, supervise, and coordinate audits and investigations relating to agency programs and operations. The Chief Financial Officers Act of 1990 established agency chief financial officers to oversee all financial management activities relating to agency programs and operations.

The Government Management Reform Act of 1994 requires the audit of agency financial statements and the preparation and audit of a consolidated financial statement for the federal government. And the Federal Financial Management Improvement Act of 1996 directs auditors to report on whether agency financial statements comply with federal financial management systems requirements, federal accounting standards, and the *U.S. Standard General Ledger (SGL).*

In 1993, Congress enacted the Government Performance and Results Act (GPRA) to improve congressional spending decisions and agency oversight through performance budgeting. GPRA holds federal agencies accountable for achieving program results and requires agencies to clarify their missions, set program goals, and measure performance toward achieving those goals. Among other things, the act requires each agency, on an annual basis, to submit a performance plan and performance report to OMB and Congress covering each program activity in the agency's budget. The agency plan must establish goals that define the level of performance to be achieved by a program activity and describe the operational processes and resources required to achieve goals. The program performance reports present the agency's performance in comparison to the plan for the previous fiscal year.

OMB reviews program and financial reports and monitors agencies' efforts to attain program objectives. Congress exercises oversight over executive branch agencies through the legislative process, formal hearings, and investigations. Congress uses oversight hearings, for example, to evaluate the effectiveness of a program and whether it is administered in a cost-effective manner, to determine whether the agency is carrying out congressional intent, and to identify fraud or abuse.

GAO regularly audits, examines, and evaluates government programs. Its findings and recommendations for corrective action are made to Congress, to OMB, and to the agencies concerned. GAO also has the authority to settle all accounts of the United States government and to issue legal decisions and opinions concerning the availability and use of appropriated funds.[14] GAO develops government audit and internal control standards. *Government Auditing Standards* (the "Yellow Book") contains standards for audits of government organizations, programs, activities, and functions, and of government assistance received by contractors, nonprofit organizations, and other nongovernmental organizations. These standards, often referred to as U.S. generally accepted government auditing standards,

---

[14] 31 U.S.C. §§ 3526, 3529.

are to be followed by auditors and audit organizations when required by law, regulation, agreement, contract, or policy. The internal control standards, *Standards for Internal Control in the Federal Government*, provide the overall framework for establishing and maintaining internal control and for identifying and addressing major performance and management challenges and areas at greatest risk for fraud and mismanagement. Also, as mentioned above, the Impoundment Control Act of 1974 requires the Comptroller General to monitor the performance of the executive branch in reporting proposed impoundments to Congress.

Chapter 3

APPENDIX II

United States Government Accountability Office

FEDERAL BUDGET FORMULATION AND APPROPRIATION PROCESSES

As described in appendix I, figure 1 shows the executive branch budget formulation process, which starts when the President develops budget and fiscal policy and concludes when the President sends the proposed budget to Congress by the first Monday in February. Congress then starts the budget and appropriations process illustrated in figure 2.

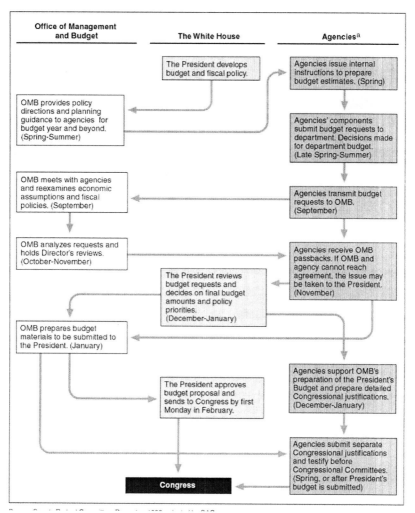

Source: Senate Budget Committee, December 1998, adapted by GAO.

[a] The term "agency" refers to either the department, agency, or lower component levels, depending on the level of decision being made. The budget submitted to OMB represents the budget decisions made at the department or the highest organizational level.

Figure 1. Federal Budget Formulation Process

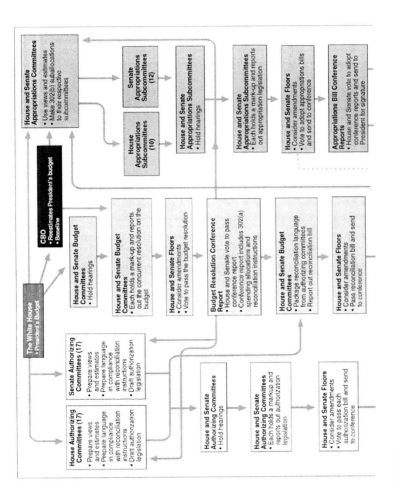

Figure 2 continued on next page

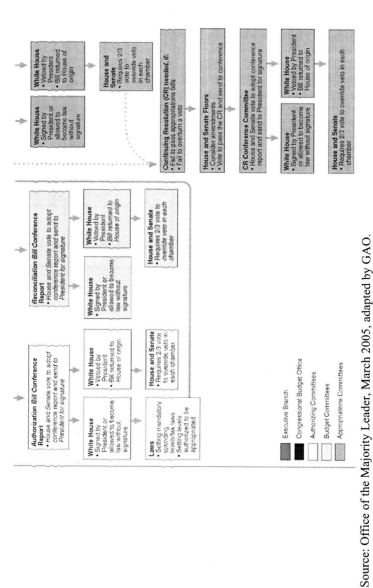

Source: Office of the Majority Leader, March 2005, adapted by GAO.

Figure 2. Federal Budget and Appropriation Process

Chapter 4

APPENDIX III

United States Government Accountability Office

THE METHODS FOR TRACKING FUNDS IN THE FEDERAL GOVERNMENT

The federal government uses two different but overlapping methods for tracking funds. This reflects the fact that the federal government is made up of many different entities and serves multiple constituencies. Financial information generated by federal entities serves a range of purposes. For example, Congress seeks to monitor the obligation and expenditure of federal funds it appropriates and evaluate the need for additional funds; managers of federal entities seek to control the cost of operations; and economists seek to understand the effects of federal operations and financing on different markets.

The two methods for tracking funds are generally known as obligational accounting and proprietary accounting. While each method involves different processes, people, and information systems that rely on a given nomenclature, each system plays an important part in ensuring the financial accountability of the government to the American people, and agencies cannot overlook either of them.

Although the budget and budget process largely use obligational accounting, users of this glossary should recognize that terms used in obligational accounting might have different meanings when used in proprietary accounting.[1] The purpose of this appendix is to describe, briefly, the two methods, their statutory bases, and the role each plays in federal government financial accountability. This appendix also supplies references for detailed information on each method. In its simplest form obligational accounting means that an obligation must be recorded when an agency enters into a contract for goods or services. In contrast, under proprietary or financial accounting no transaction is recorded until the entity accepts the goods or services when an "accounts payable" is recorded. The following paragraphs explain these two systems further.

Obligational accounting involves the accounting systems, processes, and people involved in collecting financial information necessary to control, monitor, and report on all funds made available to federal entities by legislation—including both permanent, indefinite appropriations and appropriations enacted in annual and supplemental appropriations laws that may be available for 1 or multiple fiscal years. It is through obligational accounting that agencies ensure compliance with fiscal laws, including the Antideficiency Act[2] and the "purpose" and "time" statutes.[3] Obligational accounting rests on the central concepts of the obligation and disbursement of public funds, as those terms are defined in this glossary. The Antideficiency Act and the "recording statute"[4] provide the fundamental components of obligational accounting. The Antideficiency Act requires each agency head to establish an administrative system of funds control designed to restrict obligations or expenditures and to affix responsibility for obligations or expenditures. The recording statute requires agencies to

---

[1] Some, including OMB, refer to obligational accounting as budgetary accounting. Budgetary accounting, however, more specifically refers to a bookkeeping refinement of obligational accounting. Obligational accounting is also sometimes referred to as funds control accounting or appropriation accounting. See Cornelius E. Tierney, *Handbook of Federal Accounting Practices* (Reading, Mass.: 1982). See also Senate Committee on Government Operations, Financial Management in the Federal Government, S. Doc. No. 87-11 at 85 (1961) (explaining new statute for recording obligations to support agency budget information).

[2] Codified in part at 31 U.S.C. §§ 1341, 1514, and 1517.

[3] The "purpose" statute states that "appropriations shall be applied only to the objects for which the appropriations were made." 31 U.S.C. § 1301(a). The "time" statutes relate to limits on the availability of appropriations for more than a fiscal year for a definite appropriation. 31 U.S.C. §§ 1301(c) (limitation on construing the availability of appropriations for more than a fiscal year); and 1502(a) (limitations on use of funds appropriated for obligation during a definite period).

[4] 31 U.S.C. § 1501.

account for obligations as a key mechanism for measuring compliance. The basic premise of obligational accounting is that if an agency controls its obligations, it is unlikely to overspend, or improperly use, its appropriations.

In obligational accounting, the Department of the Treasury (Treasury), in collaboration with the Office of Management and Budget (OMB), establishes federal appropriations and fund accounts to record information on the amount and period of availability of funding appropriated by acts of Congress. Imbedded in the information fields and symbols assigned by Treasury to appropriations and fund accounts are the same Treasury account symbols OMB assigns for budget accounts.[5] For additional levels of control, OMB and federal entities subdivide the appropriations and fund accounts, and then the entities record transactions in these accounts as they occur. (See Apportionment.) Treasury publishes guidance in the *Treasury Financial Manual*, available at www.fms.treas.gov/tfm/, for agencies to follow in accounting for use of funds and in preparing financial reports on their accounts.[6] Reports on the status of funds obligated and expended are periodically reported through Treasury's FACTS II and presented in a manner that is compatible with the federal budget. The Comptroller General also has statutory authority to settle the accounts of the U.S. government that involves the review and determination that obligations and disbursements from an account were made in accordance with law.[7] GAO's *Principles of Federal Appropriations Law*, available at www.gao.gov, provides a comprehensive discussion of the relevant statutes and case law, including Comptroller General decisions and opinions applicable to obligational accounting.

Proprietary accounting, also referred to as financial accounting, involves federal entities recording and accumulating financial information on transactions and balances for purposes of reporting both internally to management and externally in an entity's financial statements in accordance

---

[5] Three appropriation and fund accounts are excluded by law from the U.S. budget even though OMB assigns each a budget account symbol (i.e., U.S. Postal Service Fund and the Social Security trust fund accounts). Balances in these accounts are included as the "off-budget" component in the presentation of the total receipts and expenditures of the federal government's "unified budget."

[6] See 31 U.S.C. §§ 331 and 3513, and GAO's *Policy and Procedures Manual for Guidance of Federal Agencies, Title 7 – Fiscal Guidance*, available at www.gao.gov.

[7] 31 U.S.C. § 3526. See B-161457, August 1, 1969, for guidance on account settlement procedures.

with a comprehensive basis of accounting.[8] Proprietary accounting is usually based on generally accepted accounting principles, which follow established conventions such as the recognition of transactions on an accrual basis instead of recognition based on strict association with the obligation or expenditure of appropriated funds. For example, in proprietary accounting, the expense associated with a capital asset would be recognized over the asset's life as depreciation. In obligational or budgetary accounting, capital asset costs are recognized as obligations when the commitment to purchase the asset is made and as expenditures when cash is paid for the asset. Most federal entities are subject to proprietary accounting standards promulgated through the Federal Accounting Standards Advisory Board (FASAB).[9] FASAB was established jointly by GAO, Treasury, and OMB to promulgate accounting standards for the executive branch. The Consolidated Financial Statements of the U.S. Government, required by law to be prepared annually by Treasury and audited by GAO, are to be prepared in accordance with FASAB accounting standards.[10] All executive agencies that are not required by another provision of federal law to prepare audited financial statements are required by 31 U.S.C. § 3515 to prepare audited financial statements. Government corporations are also required to prepare audited financial statements.[11]

Most agencies and some government corporations follow FASAB accounting standards. These agencies use accounts established in the Standard General Ledger (SGL). The SGL accounts, established by Treasury and published in a chart of accounts, record similar types of transactions and balances that aggregate to specific classifications in the financial statements. The SGL accounts are structured differently than, but integrate information from, appropriations and fund accounts. Some federal entities, however,

---

[8] In the private sector, the internal system of accounting within organizations to support planning (e.g., budgeting) and decision making by managers is also known as managerial accounting or managerial cost accounting. While both systems of accounting used in the federal government contain elements of or may support managerial accounting, the federal government generally does not use such a discrete system of accounting. Federal agencies may also use other special types or applications of accounting for discrete functions or purposes carried out under their cognizance. For example, the Board of Governors of the Federal Reserve System publishes national economic data in its quarterly *Flow of Funds Accounts of the United States*. See www.federalreserve.gov/releases/ Z1. See also Statement of Federal Financial Accounting Standards No. 4, *Managerial Cost Accounting Standards*.

[9] See www.fasab.gov.

[10] 31 U.S.C. § 331(e).

[11] 31 U.S.C. §§ 9101 *et seq.*

such as government corporations, may follow other generally accepted proprietary accounting standards (such as those issued by the Financial Accounting Standards Board) unless they chose to adopt FASAB standards and the SGL. Other small federal entities, such as boards and commissions, and some legislative and judicial branch entities may not engage in proprietary accounting.

The differences between obligational accounting and proprietary accounting are most apparent in their application to federal entities' transactions, as the following hypothetical text illustrates:

> When an agency official enters into a contract for goods or services, obligational accounting rules dictate that the entity record an obligation of federal funds that will be due for the expected payment. An expenditure is recorded when payment is made (typically, after acceptance of the goods or services). Under proprietary accounting, no transaction is recorded until the entity accepts the goods or services, at which point an account payable and related expense will be recorded.

As illustrated above, each method of tracking funds serves a different purpose, and users need to be cognizant of the different purposes and the different views that these systems provide regarding federal entities' status of funds and financial condition at any given point in time.

Chapter 5

APPENDIX IV

United States Government Accountability Office

BUDGET FUNCTIONAL CLASSIFICATION

The functional classification system is a way of grouping budgetary resources so that all budget authority and outlays of on-budget and off-budget federal entities and tax expenditures can be presented according to the national needs being addressed. National needs are grouped in 17 broad areas to provide a coherent and comprehensive basis for analyzing and understanding the budget. Three additional categories—Net Interest, Allowances, and Undistributed Offsetting Receipts—do not address specific national needs but are included to cover the entire budget. A final category, Multiple Functions, is used for accounts that involve two or more major functions.

To the extent feasible, functional classifications are made without regard to agency or organizational distinctions.[1] Each federal activity is placed in a single functional classification that best defines the activity's most important purpose even though many activities serve more than one purpose. This is

---

[1] For a graphic display of budget functions by agency and object class, see GAO, *Federal Budget: Agency Obligations by Budget Function and Object Classification for Fiscal Year 2003*, GAO-04-834 (Washington, D.C.: June 25, 2004).

Table 1. Functional Classification Structure

Code	Subcode	Function or subfunction
050		National Defense
		Common defense and security of the United States. It encompasses the • raising, equipping, and maintaining of armed forces (including civilian support activities), development and utilization of weapons systems (including nuclear weapons), and related programs; • direct compensation and benefits paid to active military and civilian personnel and contributions to their retirement, health, and life insurance funds;[a] • defense research, development, testing, and evaluation; and • procurement, construction, stockpiling, and other activities undertaken to directly foster national security.
		Excludes • benefits or compensation to veterans and their dependents and military and civil service retirees; • the peaceful conduct of foreign relations; • foreign military, economic, and humanitarian assistance; • subsidies to businesses by civilian agencies (such as maritime subsidies) that may be partially justified as promoting national security; and research and operations of agencies (such as space research) whose program missions are not directly designed to promote national defense but could result in some significant benefits to our national security.
	051	Department of Defense—Military With minor exceptions, entire agency is included in this subfunction.
	053	Atomic energy defense activities Department of Energy programs devoted to national defense, such as naval ship reactors and nuclear weapons.

Table 1. Continued

Code	Subcode	Function or subfunction
	054	Defense-related activities
		Miscellaneous defense activities, such as the expenses connected with selective services and with defense stockpiles outside of the Departments of Defense and Energy.
150		International Affairs
		Maintaining peaceful relations, commerce, and travel between the United States and the rest of the world and promoting international security and economic development abroad. (Excludes outlays from domestic programs that may tangentially affect foreign relations or the citizens of other nations.)
	151	International development and humanitarian assistance
		Humanitarian assistance, development assistance, security support assistance, grants to and investments in international financial and development institutions, and the budgetary costs associated with concessionary agricultural exports.
	152	International security assistance
		The transfer of defense articles and services to foreign governments, including grants, credit sales, and training. Excludes the military sales trust fund, which is classified under subfunction 155 (international financial programs).
	153	Conduct of foreign affairs
		Diplomatic and consular operations of the Department of State, assessed contributions to international organizations, and closely related activities in other agencies (such as the Arms Control and Disarmament Agency).
	154	Foreign information and exchange activities
		Student and cultural exchange programs and foreign library, radio, or other media information activities designed to promote mutual understanding between the people of the United States and other nations.

Table 1. Continued

Code	Subcode	Function or subfunction
	155	International financial programs
		Export credit, the military sales trust fund, international commodity agreements, international monetary programs, and other programs designed to improve the functioning of the international financial system. For pre-1992 direct loans or loan guarantees, includes the total cash flows on these loans and guarantees. For loans or loan guarantees obligated or committed after 1991, includes the credit subsidy costs of the loans or guarantees.
250		General Science, Space, and Technology
		Budget resources allocated to science and research activities of the federal government that are not an integral part of the programs conducted under any other function.
		Includes the research conducted by the National Science Foundation, all space programs conducted by the National Aeronautics and Space Administration, and general science research supported by the Department of Energy. Includes research and technology programs that have diverse goals and cannot readily be classified under one specific function to avoid detailed splitting of accounts.
	251	General science and basic research
		Conducting the National Science Foundation programs and the general science activities of the Department of Energy.
	252	Space flight, research, and supporting activities
		Development and operation of space transportation systems, basic scientific research connected with outer space, research and demonstrations designed to promote terrestrial applications of technology developed through space research, and development of new space technologies for future flight missions. Also includes costs of tracking and data relay support for the National Aeronautics and Space Administration space science and applications for flight missions.

Table 1. Continued

Code	Subcode	Function or subfunction
270		Energy
		Promoting an adequate supply and appropriate use of energy to serve the needs of the economy. Included are the energy programs of the Department of Energy and its predecessor agencies. Excludes atomic energy defense activities and general science research not closely related to energy.
	271	Energy supply
		Increasing the supply of energy through the development of domestic resources and systems capable of using them. Includes the costs of research and demonstration of supply systems.
	272	Energy conservation
		Encouraging the prudent use of energy resources.
	274	Emergency energy preparedness
		Developing and maintaining a stockpile of energy resources (currently confined to petroleum) to meet emergency needs and associated contingency planning activities.
	276	Energy information, policy, and regulation
		Unallocable overhead activities of the Department of Energy plus the costs of energy information and regulation activities.
300		Natural Resources and Environment
		Developing, managing, and maintaining the nation's natural resources and environment. Excludes the outlays for community water supply programs, basic sewer systems, and waste treatment plants, all of which are part of a community or regional development (rather than an environmental enhancement) program or are part of the cost of operating a federal facility (such as a military installation).

Table 1. Continued

Code	Subcode	Function or subfunction
	301	Water resources
		Water protection, conservation, irrigation, and related activities, including the total costs of multipurpose water projects where it is not feasible to separate the transportation (navigation) or energy (power) segments of these projects.
	302	Conservation and land management
		Maintaining the public domain and national forests, encouraging conservation of private land, and reclaiming surface mining areas.
	303	Recreational resources
		Acquisition, improvement, and operation of recreational lands and facilities, including fish, wildlife, and parks; also preserving historic areas.
	304	Pollution control and abatement
		Controlling and reducing air, water, and land pollution, or enhancing the environment. Excludes water resources programs, water treatment plants, and similar programs that are not funded as part of an environmental enhancement activity.
	306	Other natural resources
		Miscellaneous natural resources programs, not classified under other subfunctions, such as marine-, earth-, and atmosphere-related research and geological surveys and mapping.
350		Agriculture
		Promoting the economic stability of agriculture and the nation's capability to maintain and increase agricultural production. Excludes programs that though related to rural development, are not directly related to agriculture, such as rural environmental and conservation programs classified in the natural resources function. Also excludes concessionary food export sales or food donations, whether overseas or for domestic income support purposes.

Table 1. Continued

Code	Subcode	Function or subfunction
	351	Farm income stabilization
		Subsidies and other payments to stabilize agricultural prices at an equitable level. Includes acquiring and storing agricultural commodity stockpiles, but does not include foreign agricultural export losses (classified in the international affairs function) or domestic donations of food (part of an income support, rather than a farm price support, program). Includes the total cash flows of farm price support loans (that is, loans that can be repaid in cash or by surrendering title to the crop used as security for the loan), which are not subject to credit reform. For all other agricultural loans and loan guarantees, includes either the total cash flows (for pre-1992 loans and loan guarantees) or the subsidy cost (for loans and loan guarantees subject to credit reform).
	352	Agricultural research and services
		All other agricultural programs, such as agricultural research and extension services.
370		Commerce and Housing Credit
		• collection and dissemination of social and economic data (unless they are an integral part of another function, such as health); • general purpose subsidies to businesses, including credit subsidies to the housing industry (for programs subject to credit reform, includes only the credit subsidy costs of loans and loan guarantees); and • the Postal Service fund and general fund subsidies of that fund.

Table 1. Continued

Code	Subcode	Function or subfunction
		In general, includes credit and insurance programs; however, if such programs are a means of achieving the basic objectives of another function and are an integral part of the programs of that function, they are classified under the other function. Excludes regional economic development programs, even if they use credit or insurance to achieve a community development objective. Also excludes other insurance or loan programs (such as railroad loans) that are an integral part of other functions.
	371	Mortgage credit
		Includes the cash transactions for homeownership and related loan and insurance programs for pre-credit reform activity; under credit reform, includes the credit subsidy cost of any homeownership loans or guarantees.
	372	Postal Service
		Any net outlays of the Postal Service included in the budget (or off-budget).
	373	Deposit insurance
		Insurance programs protecting deposits in certain financial institutions; programs to resolve failed institutions. Deposit insurance activities are not subject to credit reform, so the budget records the cash flows for deposit insurance rather than their subsidy values.
	376	Other advancement of commerce
		Loan programs to aid specialized forms of business (such as small business) that are not included elsewhere in the functional structure. For such transactions undertaken prior to credit reform, includes the total cash flows. For activities under credit reform, includes the credit subsidy cost of the loans or guarantees. Also includes collecting and disseminating economic and demographic statistics (such as census data) and regulating business.

Table 1. Continued

Code	Subcode	Function or subfunction
400		Transportation
		Providing for the transportation of the general public, its property, or both, regardless of whether local or national and regardless of the particular mode of transportation. Includes • construction of facilities; • purchase of equipment; • research, testing, and evaluation; • provision of communications directly related to transportation (for example, air traffic control by the Federal Aviation Administration); • operating subsidies for transportation facilities (such as airports) and industries (such as railroads); and • regulatory activities directed specifically toward the transportation industry rather than toward business.
		Excludes • moving personnel or equipment as part of the operation of other government services; • foreign economic assistance that may involve assisting transportation facilities or programs abroad; • the construction of roads or trails as an integral part of the operation of public lands, parks, forests, or military reservations, unless they are specifically funded as a part of a broader transportation program; • the construction of roads or other transportation facilities as an integral part of a broad community facility or regional development program where the clear intent of the program is regional development and the provision of transportation facilities is only an incidental by-product or means to attain the objective of regional development; and • research and technology activities devoted to space research (except aeronautical technology), even though this research may eventually benefit general transportation.

Table 1. Continued

Code	Subcode	Function or subfunction
	401	Ground transportation
		Aid, and/or regulation of both for the various components of ground transportation, such as roads and highways, railroads, and urban mass transit.
	402	Air transportation
		Aid for and/or regulation of air transportation, including aeronautical research conducted by the National Aeronautics and Space Administration.
	403	Water transportation
		Aid for and/or regulation of maritime commerce.
	407	Other transportation
		General transportation programs and overhead not readily allocable to any of the preceding subfunctions.
450		Community and Regional Development
		Development of physical facilities or financial infrastructures designed to promote viable community economies. Includes transportation facilities developed as an integral part of a community development program (rather than a transportation program). Usually excludes aids to businesses unless such aids promote the economic development of depressed areas and are not designed to promote particular lines of business for their own sake. Usually excludes human development and services programs.
	451	Community development
		Grants and related programs designed to aid largely urban community development. Includes community development block grants and predecessor activities, such as the urban renewal and model cities programs. These programs are generally carried out by the Department of Housing and Urban Development.

Table 1. Continued

Code	Subcode	Function or subfunction
	452	Area and regional development
		Grants, loans, subsidies, and related aids for the economic development of depressed areas. For pre-credit reform loans, includes the total cash flows of the loans; for loans under credit reform, includes the credit subsidy cost of the loans. All these aids are generally for rural areas or are more regional than the community development programs. Area and regional development programs are generally carried out by agencies other than the Department of Housing and Urban Development, such as the Farmers Home Administration, Economic Development Administration, and Bureau of Indian Affairs.
	453	Disaster relief and insurance
		Helping communities and families recover from natural disasters.
500		Education, Training, Employment, and Social Services
		Promoting the extension of knowledge and skills, enhancing employment and employment opportunities, protecting workplace standards, and providing services to the needy. Excludes education or training undertaken as an integral part of the achievement of other functions (such as training military personnel; veterans education, training, and rehabilitation; or training of health workers in a health program). Nutrition or food service programs funded separately from social services or education are not part of this function—they are classified as income security.
	501	Elementary, secondary, and vocational education
		Preschool, elementary, secondary, and vocational education programs.
	502	Higher education
		College and graduate school programs.
	503	Research and general education aids
		Education research and assistance for the arts, the humanities, educational radio and television, public libraries, and museums.

Table 1. Continued

Code	Subcode	Function or subfunction
	504	Training and employment
		Job or skill training, employment services and placement, and payments to employers to subsidize employment.
	505	Other labor services
		Aids to or regulation of the labor market, including gathering labor statistics and mediation and conciliation services; excludes employment and training programs and occupational safety and health programs.
	506	Social services
		Programs that provide a broad range of services to individuals to help them improve their vocational capabilities (such as vocational rehabilitation) or family status; services to the poor and elderly that are not primarily for income support and that are not an integral part of some other function (such as social services block grants).
550		Health
		Programs other than Medicare whose basic purpose is to promote physical and mental health, including the prevention of illness and accidents. Excludes the Medicare program, the largest federal health program, which by law is in a separate function (function 570). Also excludes federal health care for military personnel (051) and veterans (703). Also excludes general scientific research that has medical applications (such as that conducted by the National Science Foundation) and health programs financed through foreign assistance programs.
	551	Health care services
		Medical services to individuals and families, whether such services are provided directly by the federal government or financed through grants, contracts, insurance, or reimbursements.
	552	Health research and training
		All research programs—whether basic or applied—that are financed specifically as health or medical research. Excludes research that is an integral part of other functions (such as biomedical research in the space program).

Table 1. Continued

Code	Subcode	Function or subfunction
	554	Consumer and occupational health and safety
		Meat and poultry inspection, food and drug inspection, consumer product safety, and occupational health and safety.
570		Medicare
		Federal hospital insurance and federal supplementary medical insurance, along with general fund subsidies of these funds and associated offsetting receipts.
	571	Medicare
		Entire Medicare function.
600		Income Security
		Support payments (including associated administrative expenses) to persons for whom no current service is rendered. Includes retirement, disability, unemployment, welfare, and similar programs, except for Social Security and income security for veterans, which are in other functions. Also includes the Food Stamp, Special Milk, and Child Nutrition programs (whether the benefits are in cash or in kind); both federal and trust fund unemployment compensation and workers' compensation; public assistance cash payments; benefits to the elderly and to coal miners; and low- and moderate-income housing benefits. Excludes (1) financial assistance for education, (2) medical care (whether in cash or in kind), (3) subsidies to businesses (such as farm price supports), and (4) reimbursement for child care services, even though any of these may end up as income to persons. Also excludes income security programs included in the Social Security function (function 650) and programs restricted to veterans and their dependents.
	601	General retirement and disability insurance (excluding Social Security)
		Non-needs-tested retirement and disability programs composed mainly of the Railroad Retirement Fund and special benefits for coal miners. Excludes programs specifically restricted to federal employees.

Table 1. Continued

Code	Subcode	Function or subfunction
	602	Federal employee retirement and disability
		All funded retirement and disability programs restricted to federal employees. Includes military retirement benefits for all years, not just the years since the military retirement program began as a funded trust fund (1985). In cases where retirement benefits are not funded (such as in the case of Coast Guard retired pay), includes the cash benefits where the employees were employed (in the Coast Guard case, transportation), because otherwise those functions would never be charged for the retirement costs of their employees.
	603	Unemployment compensation
		Benefits not conditioned by needs tests for unemployed workers. Excludes other benefits (such as food stamps) that an unemployed person might be eligible for under other programs.
	604	Housing assistance
		Federal income support and related expenses that are specifically for financing or providing housing for individuals and families. Excludes loans, loan guarantees, or insurance. (The distinction between the housing assistance included in subfunction 604 and the mortgage credit assistance in subfunction 371 is that the subfunction 604 payments focus on subsidies to increase beneficiaries' effective income, whereas the credit subsidies in subfunction 371 are primarily aimed at encouraging the housing industry.)
	605	Food and nutrition assistance
		Providing food or nutritional assistance to individuals and families.

Table 1. Continued

Code	Subcode	Function or subfunction
	609	Other income security
		Income security programs not included in any other subfunction. Primarily either direct payments or grants-in-aid to finance direct payments that constitute cash income to low-income individuals and families. Also includes refugee assistance and both administrative expenses and offsetting collections in the income security function that are not part of any other subfunction.
650		Social Security
		Federal Old-Age and Survivors and Disability Insurance Trust Funds, along with general fund subsidies of these funds and associated offsetting collections.
	651	Social Security
		Includes the entire Social Security function.
700		Veterans Benefits and Services
		Programs providing benefits and services, the eligibility for which is related to prior military service, but the financing of which is not an integral part of the costs of national defense. As a rule, the outlays in this function are similar to those in the broader general purpose functions (such as income security or health), but restricted to veterans, their dependents, and their survivors. Excludes earned rights of career military personnel that are a cost of the defense budget (such as military retired pay or medical care).
	701	Income security for veterans
		Veterans' compensation, life insurance, pensions, and burial benefits.
	702	Veterans' education, training, and rehabilitation
		Composed primarily of the "G.I. Bill" readjustment, vocational rehabilitation benefits, and related programs.
	703	Hospital and medical care for veterans
		Medical care and research financed by the Department of Veterans Affairs.

Table 1. Continued

Code	Subcode	Function or subfunction
	704	Veterans' housing
		Housing loan and guarantee programs for veterans and dependents. Pre-1992 housing loans and guarantees are recorded on a cash basis, whereas under credit reform (post-1991), the budget records the credit subsidy cost of the activity.
	705	Other veterans benefits and services
		Administrative expenses of the Department of Veterans Affairs.
750		Administration of Justice
		Programs to provide judicial services, police protection, law enforcement (including civil rights), rehabilitation and incarceration of criminals, and the general maintenance of domestic order. Includes the provision of court-appointed counsel or other legal services for individuals. Excludes the cost of the legislative branch, the police or guard activities to protect federal property, and activities that are an integral part of a broader function (such as those for postal inspectors, tax collection agents, and Park Service rangers). The cost of National Guard personnel and military personnel who are called upon occasionally to maintain public safety and the cost of military police are included under the national defense function rather than this function.
	751	Federal law enforcement activities
		The costs of operating the Federal Bureau of Investigation, Customs and Border Protection, Immigration and Customs Enforcement, the Drug Enforcement Administration, and police and crime prevention activities in other programs. Also includes the readily identifiable enforcement cost of civil rights activities
	752	Federal litigative and judicial activities
		The cost of the judiciary, the cost of prosecution, and federal expenses connected with financing legal defense activities.

Table 1. Continued

Code	Subcode	Function or subfunction
	753	Federal correctional activities
		Covers the costs of incarceration, supervision, parole, and rehabilitation of federal prisoners.
	754	Criminal justice assistance
		Grants to state and local governments to assist them in operating and improving their law enforcement and justice systems.
800		General Government
		General overhead cost of the federal government, including legislative and executive activities; provision of central fiscal, personnel, and property activities; and provision of services that cannot reasonably be classified in any other major function. As a rule, all activities reasonably or closely associated with other functions are included in those functions rather than being listed as part of general government. Also includes shared revenues and other general purpose fiscal assistance.
	801	Legislative functions
		Includes most of the legislative branch. However, the Library of Congress (except the Congressional Research Service), the Tax Court, the Government Printing Office (except for congressional printing and binding), and the Copyright Royalty Tribunal are classified in other subfunctions.
	802	Executive direction and management
		The Executive Office of the President (unless some major grants or operating programs should be included in the Office); occasionally some closely related spending outside the Office is included.
	803	Central fiscal operations
		Covers the general tax collection and fiscal operations of the Department of the Treasury.
	804	General property and records management
		Most of the operations of the General Services Administration (net of reimbursements from other agencies for services rendered).

Table 1. Continued

Code	Subcode	Function or subfunction
	805	Central personnel management
		Most of the operating costs of the Office of Personnel Management and related agencies (net of reimbursements from other agencies for services rendered).
	806	General purpose fiscal assistance
		Federal aid to state, local, and territorial governments that is available for general fiscal support. The transactions of the now discontinued general revenue-sharing program are included in the historical data for this subfunction. Also includes grants for more restricted purposes when the stipulated purposes cross two or more major budgetary functions and the distribution among those functions is at the discretion of the recipient jurisdiction rather than the federal government. Includes payments in lieu of taxes, broad-purpose shared revenues, and the federal payment to the District of Columbia. Excludes payments specifically for community development or social services programs.
	808	Other general government
		Miscellaneous other costs, such as federal costs of territorial governments.
	809	Deductions for offsetting receipts
		Includes general government function offsetting receipts that are not closely related to any other subfunction in this function.
900		Net Interest
		Transactions that directly give rise to interest payments or income (lending) and the general shortfall or excess of outgo over income arising out of fiscal, monetary, and other policy considerations and leading to the creation of interest-bearing debt instruments (normally the public debt). Includes interest paid on the public debt, on uninvested funds, and on tax refunds, offset by interest collections.
	901	Interest on the Treasury debt securities (gross)
		Outlays for interest on the public debt. (Where this interest is paid to the public, it is on an accrual basis; all other interest outlays in the budget are on a cash basis.)

Table 1. Continued

Code	Subcode	Function or subfunction
	902	Interest received by on-budget trust funds
		Interfund interest collected by on-budget nonrevolving trust funds. Most of this income derives from outlays included in subfunction 901, but this subfunction also includes offsetting receipts from investments in public debt securities issued by the Federal Financing Bank (FFB).
	903	Interest received by off-budget trust funds
		Interfund interest collected by off-budget nonrevolving trust funds. Normally, all of this income comes from outlays included in subfunction 901.
	908	Other interest
		All other interest expenditures and offsetting receipts. The principal expenditure in this subfunction normally is interest on refunds of receipts. Since offsetting interest receipts are included in this subfunction, the subfunction totals are usually negative.
	909	Other investment income
		The actual and estimated earnings on private securities of the Railroad Retirement Investment Trust. The actual year returns include interest, dividends, and capital gains and losses on private equities and other securities. The trust's end-of-year balance reflects the current market value of resources available to the government to finance benefits.
	920	Allowances
		A category that may be included in a budget to ensure that the budget reflects the total estimated budget authority and outlay requirements for future years.
		In addition to the budget authority and outlays in each of the functional classifications, the President's budget normally includes some budget authority and outlays classified as allowances.
	921-929	Contingencies for specific requirements
		The specific line entries will vary from budget to budget, depending on what projections are required.

Table 1. Continued

Code	Subcode	Function or subfunction
950		Undistributed Offsetting Receipts
		Most offsetting receipts are included as deductions from outlays in the applicable functions and subfunctions. However, there are five major categories of offsetting receipts that are classified as undistributed offsetting receipts rather than being included as offsets in any of the other functions.
	951	Employer share, employee retirement (on-budget)
		Employing agency payments to funded retirement systems of federal employees are intragovernmental transactions (that is, they are payments by government accounts collected by other government accounts) and, hence, both the payment and collection are included in federal outlays. The payments are included in the various agency outlays, while the offsets are undistributed.[b]
		Most federal employees are now covered by the Hospital Insurance portion of the Medicare program. The employing agency payments to the Hospital Insurance fund are also offset in this subfunction.
	952	Employer share, employee retirement (off-budget)
		Includes collections similar in nature to those in subfunction 951, except that the accounts collecting the money are off-budget.
	953	Rents and royalties on the outer continental shelf
		Rents and royalties on the outer continental shelf constitute a large source of nontax income that is largely a windfall to the government. Since there are no major government programs that give rise to this income, it would be inappropriate to offset it against the outlays in any function. Thus, the collections are undistributed.
	954	Sale of major assets
		On occasion, the government derives large returns from the sale of major assets, and the proceeds of the sales are recorded in this category rather than in any major function.

Table 1. Continued

Code	Subcode	Function or subfunction
	959	Other undistributed offsetting receipts
		This category includes items such as collections for the lease of federal lands for petroleum exploitation and a proposal for the Federal Communications Commission to conduct auctions.
Multifunction Account		
	999	Multifunction account (used for accounts that involve two or more major functions).

Source: GAO.

[a]For years prior to 1985, when the military retirement trust fund began, the historical data included imputed accruals for retirement, with a matching imputed undistributed offsetting collection (subfunction 951). The cash retirement benefits for all years are included in the income security function.[b]The historical data for this category for years prior to 1985 include an offset equal to the imputed accrual for military retirement that is included in subfunction 051. These imputations were calculated so that the data for the years prior to the creation of the military retirement trust fund would be as comparable as feasible with the subsequent years.

necessary so that the sum of the functional categories equals the budget totals. The functional classifications are also the categories that Congress uses in the concurrent resolutions on the budget, pursuant to the Congressional Budget and Impoundment Control Act of 1974 (2 U.S.C. § 632). Different programs within a single function may fall under the jurisdiction of different committees.

A function may be divided into one or more subfunctions, depending upon the complexity of the national need addressed by that function. A three-digit code represents each functional/subfunctional category. The functional codes also make up the last three digits of the account identification code. (See app. V.)

The functional structure is relatively stable, but changes are made from time to time to take into account changing conditions and requirements. As a rule, any changes in this structure are made after the Office of Management and Budget (OMB) consults with the Appropriations and Budget Committees of the Senate and House of Representatives.

Table 1 outlines the functional classification structure as taken from the President's *Budget of the United States Government, Fiscal Year 2006.* The definitions for the subfunctional structure are from OMB's technical staff paper, "The Functional Classification in the Budget" (1979 Revision). Where necessary, these definitions have been updated to accommodate changes since issuance of that document. The three-digit numbers listed under Code and the associated titles and definitions are for the major functions. The three-digit numbers listed under Subcode and the associated titles and definitions are for the subfunctions.

Chapter 6

APPENDIX V

United States Government Accountability Office

FEDERAL BUDGET ACCOUNT IDENTIFICATION CODE

Each account, or group of accounts in the President's budget is assigned an account identification code by the Office of Management and Budget (OMB), in consultation with the Department of the Treasury (Treasury). These codes are used to store and access data in the budget database, run computer reports, and identify accounts in OMB and Treasury documents and computer reports. The budget schedules that are included in the Budget Appendix volume of the President's budget use an 11-digit account identification code that is based on the following coding system (see table 2.)

An alternate 13-digit identification code is also used by OMB to access data in the budget database and generate computer reports. This code substitutes a 3-digit agency code[1] and a 2-digit bureau code assigned by OMB for the 2-digit agency code assigned by Treasury. (The bureau code is used to designate subordinate units within a department or agency.) The alternate OMB code was developed to facilitate the sequencing of information by agency and subordinate unit within the agency. (See fig. 3.)

---

[1] OMB agency codes are not the same as Treasury agency codes.

Table 2. Federal Budget Account Identification Code

Digits	Explanation
XX-xxxx-x-x-xxx	Treasury agency code—The first two digits designate the agency code as assigned by Treasury. The term "agency" refers to departments, independent agencies, and instrumentalities of the U.S. government.
xx-XXXX-x-x-xxx	Account symbol—Each account has an agency-unique number assigned by Treasury, or, in the case of merged or consolidated accounts, by OMB, that corresponds to the fund type.
xx-xxxx-X-x-xxx	Transmittal code—One-digit code that identifies the nature or timing of the associated schedules, as follows: 0=Regular budget schedules 1=Supplemental proposals 2=Legislative proposals requiring authorizing legislation that 2=are not subject to pay-as-you-go (PAYGO) 3=Appropriations language to be transmitted later; used when language for a significant policy proposal cannot be transmitted in the budget 4=Legislative proposals requiring authorizing legislation that have a PAYGO effect 5=Rescission proposal 9=Reserved for OMB use
xx-xxxx-x-**X**-xxx	Fund code—One-digit code that identifies the type of fund, as follows: 1=General fund 2=Special fund 3=Public enterprise revolving fund 4=Intragovernmental revolving or management fund 7=Trust non-revolving fund 8=Trust revolving fund
xx-xxxx-x-x-**XXX**	Subfunction code—Three-digit code that corresponds to the account's subfunctional classification. (See app. III for a further explanation of subfunctions.)

Source: GAO.

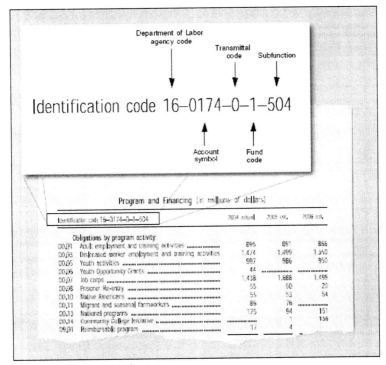

Source: GAO representation of OMB data.

Figure 3. Federal Budget Account Identification Code Digits

APPENDIX VI

United States Government Accountability Office

PROGRAM AND FINANCING SCHEDULE

The Program and Financing (PandF) schedule for each budget account appears in the *Appendix* of the President's budget (see example in fig. 4). In a standard format, it provides basic information about obligations, budget authority, and outlays for the account. Part A in figure 4 shows the information that precedes the PandF schedule. The numbers on specific features mentioned in part A are explained below:

1. The account name and the President's proposed language for the budget year's appropriation act (fiscal year 2006 in the example) related to the account appear at the top.

2. The language of the previous year's appropriation act is used as a base. Brackets enclose material proposed for deletion.

3. Italic type indicates new proposed language. When a regular appropriation has not been enacted at the time the budget is prepared, the Office of Management and Budget (OMB) may print only the language related to the fiscal year in question, in italics with no brackets shown.

4. At the end of the final appropriation language paragraph, and printed in italics within parentheses, are citations to relevant

authorizing legislation and to the appropriation act from which the basic text of the language is taken.

An 11-digit identification code, found at the top of the PandF schedule, facilitates computer processing of budgetary information. (See app. VI.)

The PandF schedule, part B in figure 4, consists of eight sections. The numbered sections contained in part B are described in detail after the figure.

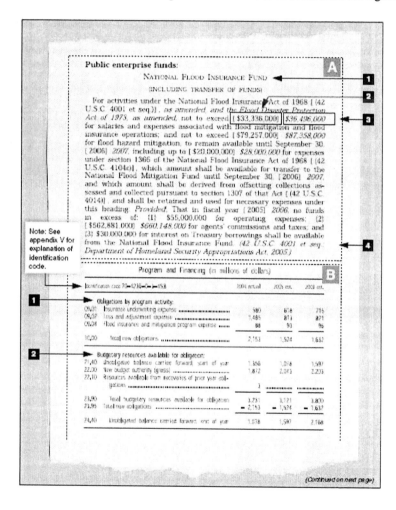

(Continued on next page)

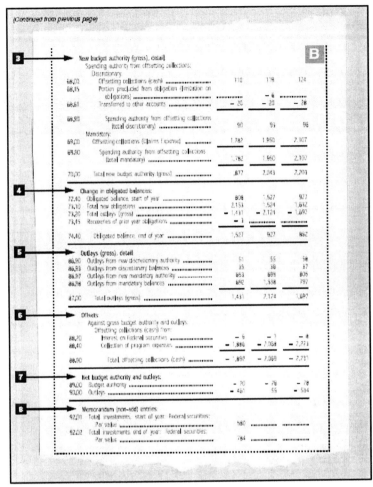

Source: GAO representation of OMB data.

Figure 4. Example of PandF Schedule Preceded by Appropriations Language for National Flood Insurance Fund Account

1. *Obligations by program activity.* Shows obligations for specific activities or projects. To provide a meaningful presentation of information for the program being financed, the activity structure is developed individually for each appropriation or fund account. That structure is tailored to the individual account and is not uniform across the government. According to OMB, the activities should clearly indicate the services to be performed or the programs to be

conducted; finance no more than one strategic goal or objective; distinguish investment, development, grant and subsidy, and operating programs; and relate to administrative control and operation of the agency. The last entry, "total new obligations," indicates the minimum amount of budgetary resources that must be available to the appropriation or fund account in that year.

2. *Budgetary resources available for obligation.* Lists detailed information on the new budget authority in the account, the unobligated balances of budgetary resources (that have not expired) brought forward from the end of the prior year, and adjustments to those amounts. The end-of-year unobligated balance is obtained by deducting new obligations and expiring amounts.

3. *New budget authority (gross) detail.* Indicates the type of budget authority (i.e. appropriations, contract authority, and spending authority from offsetting collections) and whether the authority is discretionary (controlled by appropriations acts) or mandatory (controlled by other laws).

4. *Change in obligated balances.* Offers a bridge between the start and end of the year's obligated balances. In this section, new obligations are added to previous years' unliquidated obligations. Gross outlays are subtracted from this amount. Adjustments such as transfers of obligated balances and changes in uncollected customer payments from federal sources, are added or subtracted, as appropriate, to determine the obligated balance at year-end. Transactions in unexpired accounts as well as outlays from and adjustments in expired (but not canceled) accounts are also reported.

5. *Outlays (gross), detail.* Shows the account's gross outlays distributed on the basis of the type of the budget authority that financed the outlay. This section separately presents outlays from discretionary and mandatory budget authority and outlays from new authority and carryover balances.

6. *Offsets.* Shows the offsets to gross budget authority and outlays used to arrive at net budget authority and outlays for the account. Gross outlays are reduced by cash collections (both unexpired and expired), while gross budget authority is reduced by cash collections (unexpired only) and orders from federal sources that are not accompanied by cash. The offsets section indicates the source of the offsetting collections (such as federal sources, interest on federal securities, and nonfederal sources). The change in uncollected customer payments from federal sources from the start

to the end of the year is deducted from gross budget authority only. Increases in uncollected customer payments from the start to the end of the year increase the amount of the offset because the increase constitutes an increase in gross budget authority. Decreases reduce the amount of the offset because a decrease means that a portion of the offsetting collections (cash) received has been applied to liquidate obligations for which an offset was already counted. Only unexpired offsetting collections (cash) are offset from gross budget authority because gross budget authority includes only unexpired amounts.

7. *Net budget authority and outlays.* Shows the amount available for new obligation net of the offsetting collections attributable to unexpired offsets. Net budget authority is equal to gross budget authority minus cash collections (unexpired only) and orders from federal sources that are not accompanied by cash. Net outlays are equal to gross outlays minus cash collections (both unexpired and expired).

8. *Memorandum (non-add) entries.* May include obligations in excess of available budgetary resources, investments in federal securities, and balances of contract authority. The amounts are not added or deducted from the budget authority or outlay amounts.

APPENDIX VII

United States Government Accountability Office

OBJECT CLASSIFICATION

Object classes are categories used in budget preparation to classify obligations by the items or services purchased by the federal government. The major object classes and their corresponding numbers are

10 – Personnel compensation and benefits
20 – Contractual services and supplies
30 – Acquisition of assets
40 – Grants and fixed charges
90 – Other

These object classes present obligations according to their initial purpose rather than the result or service. For example, the wage obligations of a federal employee who is paid to construct a building are classified as "Personnel compensation and benefits," but the contractual obligations for the purchase of a building are classified as "Acquisition of assets."

Obligations are recorded when the federal government places an order for an item or a service, awards a contract, receives a service, or enters into transactions that will require payments in the same or a future period. Obligations are also recorded when an expenditure transfer is made between federal government accounts. Object class information is mandated by law

(31 U.S.C. § 1104(b)), which requires the President's budget to present obligations by object class for each account.

Object class information is reported whenever obligations are reported on a program and financing schedule (except that object class information is not reported for credit financing accounts). Therefore, obligations are reported by object class separately for the regular budget requests, supplemental budget requests, rescission proposals, and legislative proposals. Object class schedules also separately identify the following types of obligations: direct and reimbursable obligations; obligations covered by statutory limitations; and obligations for allocations between agencies.

Object classes are subdivided into smaller classes. (For an example, see fig. 5.) The following table of object classification is taken from OMB Circular No. A-11:

10	Personnel Compensation and Benefits
11	Personnel compensation
11.1	Full-time permanent
11.3	Other than full-time permanent
11.5	Other personnel compensation
11.7	Military personnel
11.8	Special personal services payment
11.9	Total personnel compensation
12	Personnel benefits
12.1	Civilian personnel benefits
12.2	Military personnel benefits
13	Benefits of former personnel
20	Contractual Services and Supplies
21	Travel and transportation of persons
22	Transportation of things
23	Rent, communications, and utilities
23.1	Rental payments to the General Services Administration
23.2	Rental payments to others
23.3	Communications, utilities, and miscellaneous charges
24	Printing and reproduction
25	Other contractual services
25.1	Advisory and assistance services
25.2	Other services
25.3	Other purchases of goods and services from government accounts
25.4	Operation and maintenance of facilities
25.5	Research and development contracts
25.6	Medical care
25.7	Operation and maintenance of equipment

25.8	Subsistence and support of persons
26	Supplies and materials
30	Acquisition of Assets
31	Equipment
32	Land and structures
33	Investments and loans
40	Grants and Fixed Charges
41	Grants, subsidies, and contributions
42	Insurance claims and indemnities
43	Interest and dividends
44	Refunds
90	Other
91	Unvouchered
92	Undistributed
93	Limitation on expenses
94	Financial transfers
99	Subtotal, obligations
99.5	Below reporting threshold
99.9	Total new obligations

Object Classification (in millions of dollars)

Identification code 21-2016-0-1-051

		2004 actual	2005 est.	2006 est.
	Direct obligations:			
	Personnel compensation:			
11.7	Military personnel	26,159	20,193	20,542
11.8	Special personal services payments	1		
11.9	Total personnel compensation	26,160	20,193	20,542
12.2	Accrued retirement benefits	4,997	3,879	4,041
12.2	Other personnel benefits	2,130	2,484	2,480
12.2	Military personnel benefits	2,253	2,499	
13.0	Benefits for former personnel	273	53	152
21.0	Travel and transportation of persons	660	341	229
22.0	Transportation of things	354	576	774
25.3	Other purchases of goods and services from Government accounts	724		
25.7	Operation and maintenance of equipment	28	31	66
25.8	Subsistence and support of persons	805	149	
26.0	Supplies and materials	1,960	110	132
42.0	Insurance claims and indemnities	13	3	7
43.0	Interest and dividends	0		
99.0	Direct obligations	40,363	30,324	28,402
99.0	Reimbursable obligations	496	288	297
99.9	Total new obligations	40,859	30,612	28,699

Source: GAO representation of OMB data.

Figure 5. Example of Object Classification for Department of Defense Program

IMAGE SOURCES

This section contains credit and copyright information for images and graphics in this product, as appropriate, when that information was not listed adjacent to the image or graphic.

Front cover clockwise:
PhotoDisc (Treasury)
Eyewire (White House)
GAO (capitol)

GAO's Mission	The Government Accountability Office, the audit, evaluation and investigative arm of Congress, exists to support Congress in meeting its constitutional responsibilities and to help improve the performance and accountability of the federal government for the American people. GAO examines the use of public funds; evaluates federal programs and policies; and provides analyses, recommendations, and other assistance to help Congress make informed oversight, policy, and funding decisions. GAO's commitment to good government is reflected in its core values of accountability, integrity, and reliability.
Obtaining Copies of GAO Reports and Testimony	The fastest and easiest way to obtain copies of GAO documents at no cost is through GAO's Web site (www.gao.gov). Each weekday, GAO posts newly released reports, testimony, and correspondence on its Web site. To have GAO e-mail you a list of newly posted products every afternoon, go to www.gao.gov and select "Subscribe to Updates."
Order by Mail or Phone	The first copy of each printed report is free. Additional copies are $2 each. A check or money order should be made out to the Superintendent of Documents. GAO also accepts VISA and Mastercard. Orders for 100 or more copies mailed to a single address are discounted 25 percent. Orders should be sent to: U.S. Government Accountability Office 441 G Street NW, Room LM Washington, D.C. 20548 To order by Phone: Voice: (202) 512-6000 TDD: (202) 512-2537 Fax: (202) 512-6061

To Report Fraud, Waste, and Abuse in Federal Programs	Contact: Web site: www.gao.gov/fraudnet/fraudnet.htm E-mail: fraudnet@gao.gov Automated answering system: (800) 424-5454 or (202) 512-7470
Congressional Relations	Gloria Jarmon, Managing Director, JarmonG@gao.gov (202) 512-4400 U.S. Government Accountability Office, 441 G Street NW, Room 7125 Washington, D.C. 20548
Public Affairs	Paul Anderson, Managing Director, AndersonP1@gao.gov (202) 512-4800 U.S. Government Accountability Office, 441 G Street NW, Room 7149 Washington, D.C. 20548

INDEX